MW01037932

CogAT®
GRADE 2 PRACTICE TEST
FORM 7
LEVEL 8

ISBN: 978-1-948255-00-4

Origins Publications
New York, NY, USA

Email:info@originspublications.com

Origins Publications

The CogAT®Test Prep Experts help students develop their higher-order thinking skills while also improving their chances of admission into gifted and accelerated-learner programs.

Our goal is to unleash and nurture the genius in every student. We do this by offering educational and test prep materials that are fun, challenging and provide a sense of accomplishment.

Please contact us with any questions.

info@originspublications.com

Contents

Part 1.Introduction to the CogAT®

This book offers an overview of the types of questions on the CogAT® Level 8, test-taking strategies to improve performance, sample questions, and a full-length practice CogAT that students can use to assess their knowledge and practice their test-taking skills.

Who Takes the CogAT® Level 8?

There are ten CogAT levels, which are based on age.
The CogAT Level 8 is often used as an assessment tool or admissions test in 2nd grade for entry into 3rd grade of gifted and talented (GATE) programs and highly-competitive schools.

The CogAT Level 8 is also used as an assessment tool by teachers to figure out which students would benefit from an accelerated or remedial curriculum.

What is the Difference Between CogAT® Form 6 and Form 7?

The latest version of the CogAT is Form 7, published in 2011. Form 6 is still in use in some schools. Form 7 is very similar to Form 6, although some key changes have occurred.

Most importantly, Form 7 for K-2 uses pictures so the test can also be given to non English speaking students. The only words on these tests appear in the Sentence Completion questions (see below for more information and in the directions, which can be read in English or in Spanish.

When Does the CogAT® Take Place?

This depends on the school district you reside in or want to attend. Check with the relevant school/district to learn more about test dates and the application/ registration process.

CogAT® Level 8 Overview

The CogAT® is a group-administered test that features three independent 'batteries': Verbal, Quantitative, and Nonverbal. It is designed to assess learned reasoning in these three areas, which experts believe are the areas most closely linked to academic achievement. One, two, or all three batteries may be administered based on the specific needs of the test user. The CogAT® covers topics that students may not see in school, so kids will need to think a little differently in order to do well. A students stress management and time management skills are also tested during the exam.

Length

Students are given about 37-45 minutes to complete ONE battery in the CogAT Level 8 test. Children taking the Level 8 can be given each battery separately or all at the same time. A test administrator provides directions and controls pacing throughout the test. Including administration time, the CogAT 8 (all three batteries) will take between 2.5-3.5 hours

Format

The test is a black and white picture-based exam. The entire test is made up of 154 multiple choice questions. The questions are distributed as follows:

Verbal Battery		Quantitative Battery	
Sentence Completion	18	Number Analogies	18
Picture Classifications	18	Number Series	18
Picture Analogies	18	Number Puzzles	14
Non-Verbal Battery			
Figure Matrices	18		
Figure Classification	18	Total Questions 154	
Paper Folding	14		

Test Sections

The test consists of verbal, nonverbal material and quantitative material.

VERBAL BATTERY

The verbal battery on the CogAT® is designed to measure a student's vocabulary, memory, ability to solve verbal problems, and ability to determine word relationships.

This battery has three subtests, which vary depending on age.

✓ **Sentence Completion:** The administrator or teacher reads aloud a sentence with a missing word. Students select the picture that best completes the sentence.

✓ **Picture Classification:** Students are given a series of three pictures that are in some way similar. The student then selects a picture from the answer choices that is like the other three.

✓ **Picture Analogies:** Students are provided with two pictures that form a pair, as well as a third picture. From the answer choices, the student must select the picture that goes with the third provided image.

NONVERBAL BATTERY

On the nonverbal battery, students are tested on their ability to reason using geometric shapes and figures. Students must use strategies to solve unique problems that they may never have encountered in school.

The nonverbal battery is composed of three question types:

✓ Figure Classification: Students are provided with three figures and must select the fourth figure that completes the set.

✓ Figure Matrices: Students are given a 2x2 matrix with the image missing in one cell. Students must determine the relationship between the two spatial forms in the top row and find a fourth image that has the same relationship to the spatial form in the bottom row.

✓ Paper Folding: Students must determine how a hole-punched, folded paper will look once it is unfolded.

QUANTITATIVE BATTERY

The quantitative battery measures abstract reasoning, quantitative reasoning, and problem solving skills.

The quantitative battery is composed of three question types:

✓ Number Series: Students are given images of beads on an abacus. Based on the images, they must determine what the next abacus in the series should look like.

✓ Number Puzzles: Students are provided with pictures that represent math problems.

✓ Number Analogies: Students are given a 2x2 matrix with one empty cell. The student must determine the relationship between the two images in the top row, and then find the picture that has the same relationship with the image on the bottom row.

Part 2: How to Use this Book

The CogAT® is an important test and the more a student is familiar with the questions on the exam, the better she will fare when taking the test.

This book will help your child get used to the format and content of the test so s/he will be adequately prepared and feel confident on test day.

Inside this book, you will find:

- Sample question for each question type on the test and teaching tips to help your child approach each question type strategically and with confidence.

- Full-length CogAT® Level 8 practice test.

- **Access to bonus practice questions online at https://originstutoring.lpages.co/cogat-8-challenge-questions/**

Part 3. Test Prep Tips and Strategies

Firstly, and most importantly, commit to make the test preparation process a stress-free one. A student's ability to keep calm and focused in the face of challenge is a quality that will benefit her throughout her academic life.

Be prepared for difficult questions from the get-go! There will be a certain percentage of questions that are very challenging for all children. It is key to encourage students to use all strategies available when faced with challenging questions. And remember that a student can get quite a few questions wrong and still do very well on the test.

Before starting the practice test, go through the sample questions and read the teaching tips provided at the beginning of the book. They will help you guide your student as he or she progresses through the practice test.

The following strategies may also be useful as you help your child prepare:

Before You Start

Find a quiet, comfortable spot to work free of distractions.

Tell your student you will be doing some fun activities, and that this is an opportunity for you to spend some enjoyable time together.

Show your student how to perform the simple technique of shading (and erasing) bubbles.

During Prep

If your child is challenged by a question, ask your child to explain why he or she chose a specific answer. If the answer was incorrect, this will help you identify where your child is stumbling. If the answer was correct, asking your child to articulate her reasoning aloud will help reinforce the concept.

Encourage your child to carefully consider all the answer options before selecting one. Tell her there is only ONE answer.

If your child is stumped by a question, she or he can use the process of elimination. First, encourage your child to eliminate obviously wrong answers to narrow down the answer choices. If your child is still in doubt after using this technique, tell him or her to guess as there are no points deducted for wrong answers.

Review all the questions your student answered incorrectly, and explain to your student why the answer is incorrect. Have your student attempt these questions again a few days later to see if he now understands the concept.

Encourage your student to do her best, but take plenty of study breaks. Start with 10-15 minute sessions. Your student will perform best if she views these activities as fun and engaging, not as exercises to be avoided.

When to Start Preparing?

Every family and student will approach preparation for this test differently. There is no 'right' way to prepare; there is only the best way for a particular child and family. We suggest students, at minimum, take one full-length practice test and spend 6-8 hours reviewing CogAT® practice questions.

If you have limited time to prepare, spend most energy reviewing areas where your student is encountering the majority of problems.

As they say, knowledge is power! Preparing for the CogAT® will certainly help your student avoid anxiety and make sure she does not give up too soon when faced with unfamiliar and perplexing questions.

CogAT® Verbal Battery
Sample Questions & Teaching Tips

This battery includes three types of questions.

i.   Sentence Completion
ii. Picture Classifications
iii. Picture Analogies

If your child is going to go through the battery as if s/he were taking it under real testing conditions, then you should allow 40 minutes to complete this battery.

Otherwise, we suggest that your child answers each question in his or her own time, while you guide, support and give feedback as s/he progresses. In this case, we also recommend that you spend a few minutes yourself reviewing the teaching tips for each section so you can be prepared to help your student if he or she struggles with a question.

Before starting the battery, have your child try the sample questions in the next few pages.

Sentence Completion

There are 18 Sentence Completion questions in the CogAT® Level 8

Please note that the sentence completion section is optional for younger children. Check with your school or district to find out if your child will have to answer these questions types.

SAMPLE QUESTION - Read the question aloud once only.

It is the first day of school for Scott. Scott puts a snack bar, a pencil, and two books in his back pack to take to school. Which picture shows the objects in his back pack?

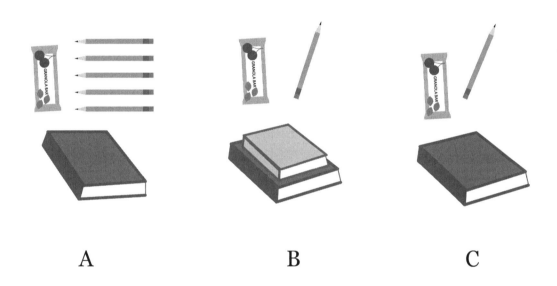

| A | B | C |

Correct Answer: B

Answer Explanation

For this question, the student must listen carefully to the sentence read aloud in order to understand and recall the list of items (a snack bar, two books, a pencil) that Scott puts in his backpack.

Option B is the only picture that shows the items described in the sentence.

Option C has one pencil and a snack bar, but only one book. Option A has a snack bar, but only one book and five pencils. Both of these are incorrect descriptions of the items that Scott put into the backpack.

TEACHING TIPS

- Tell your child to "listen carefully" before reading the question. Your child will only hear the question once in actual testing conditions, so during prep sessions it is helpful to repeat this directive before each question, as it will help your child learn the skill of paying attention and focusing on what is being said when questions are read aloud to him/her.

- Reinforce your student's understanding of relational concepts, including distinguishing between phrases such as "left" and "right", "below" and "above", and "next to" and "beside".

Picture Classifications

There are 18 Picture Classifications questions in the CogAT® Level 8

SAMPLE QUESTION

Look at the pictures in the boxes in the top row. These pictures go together in a certain way. Which picture in the bottom row goes with the pictures in the top row?

A   B   C

Correct Answer: A

Answer Explanation

In the top row, the three pictures go together because all of them are objects that have wheels.

Your child needs to find the picture among the answer options that goes together with the pictures in the top row.

Option B and C are incorrect because the objects in the pictures (a hot air balloon and a boat) do not have wheels.

Option A is correct as this is the only object that has wheels.

TEACHING TIPS

- These questions test a student's ability to identify and classify common objects into basic categories by one or more common physical property or attribute (e.g., color, size, shape, weight, liquid/solid, quantity, function). They also test knowledge of common objects and categories, such as fruits, vegetables, flowers, reptiles, mammals, jungle animals, farm animals, tools, furniture, musical instruments, eating utensils, seasons, birds, etc. Introduce these categories and characteristics in real-life situations and discuss the relationships between concepts with your student.

- Encourage your student to expand on his knowledge of a category in a question. Ask him to name other objects that share the same characteristics and belong to a specific category.

- Ask your student to explain why she chose a specific answer. This will help you identify where your student is stumbling or provide the opportunity to reinforce understanding of a category and the object/s that can "belong" to it.

Picture Analogies

There are 18 Picture Analogies questions in the CogAT® Level 8

SAMPLE QUESTION:

Which image best fits in the box with the question mark?

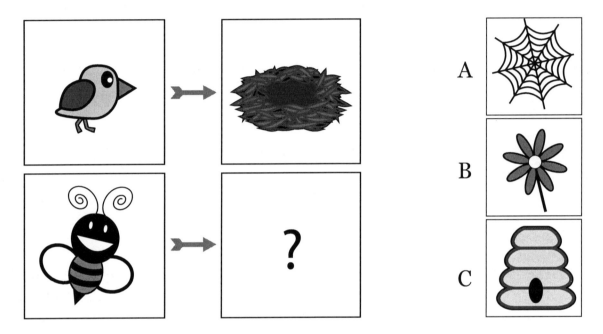

Correct Answer: C

Answer Explanation

In the top row, there are two figures that go together in the sense that a bird's home is a nest, or a bird lives in a nest.

Look at the bottom row. Your child needs to find the picture among the answer options that fits best in the question mark box on the bottom row. The correct choice has the same relationship with the picture on the left on the bottom row as the two pictures in the top row have with each other.

Option A is incorrect because a bee's home is not a web.

Option B is also incorrect as a bee's home is not a flower, even though bees like flowers.

Option C is correct because, just like a bird's home is a nest, a bee's home is a hive.

TEACHING TIPS

- To master picture analogies, a student needs to have general background knowledge, a good visual vocabulary, and an understanding/recognition of the following relationships:

  → Object/function (or reverse: function/object)

  → Agent (person or animal)/location, (or reverse: location/agent (person or animal)

  → Agent (person or animal)/object, (or reverse: object/agent (person or animal)

  → Agent (person or animal)/action, (or reverse: action/ agent (person or animal)

  → Familial -- having to do with family.

- As often as possible, incorporate discussions about similarities, differences, and relationships between words into your everyday conversation with your student. Help your student begin thinking about how different words and concepts are connected to one another.

- When answering practice questions, teach your student to determine the relationship between the first pair of pictures before looking at the answer choices. Once your student determines the relationship between the first pair, she can then look at the choices to find the pair with the exact same relationship.

CogAT® Nonverbal Battery
Sample Questions & Teaching Tips

This battery includes three types of questions.

i. Figure Classification
ii. Figure Matrices
iii. Paper Folding

If your child is going to go through the battery as if s/he were taking it under real testing conditions, then you should allow 37 minutes to complete this battery.

Otherwise, have your child answer each question in his or her own time, while you guide, support and give feedback as she progresses. Spend a few minutes reviewing the teaching tips for each section so you help your student if he struggles with a question.

Before starting the battery, ask your child to try the sample questions in the next few pages.

Figure Classification

There are 18 Figure Classification questions in the CogAT® Level 8

SAMPLE QUESTION

Look at the shapes in the top row. These shapes go together in a certain way. Which shape in the bottom row belongs with the shapes in the top row?

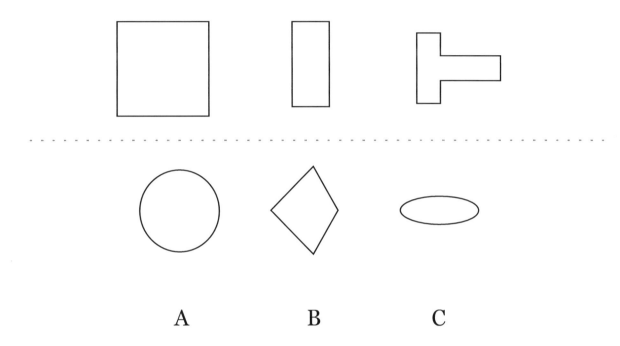

A   B   C

Correct Answer: B

Answer Explanation

In the top row, the three figures go together because all the shapes are made of straight lines. Your child needs to find the figure among the answer options that goes together with the shapes in the top row.

Option A and C are incorrect because these shapes do not have straight lines.

Option B is correct as this is the only shape that has straight lines like the shapes in the top row

TEACHING TIPS

- After your student has answered the question, encourage her to expand on her knowledge of the category in the question.

- Ask him to name or draw other objects that share the same characteristics and belong to a specific category.

- Ask your student to explain why she chose a specific answer. This will help you identify where your student is stumbling or provide the opportunity to reinforce understanding of a category and the object/s that can "belong" to it.

Figure Matrices

There are 18 Figure Matrices questions in the CogAT® Level 8

SAMPLE QUESTION:

Look at the shapes in the boxes on top. These shapes go together in a certain way. Which answer choice belongs where the question mark is?

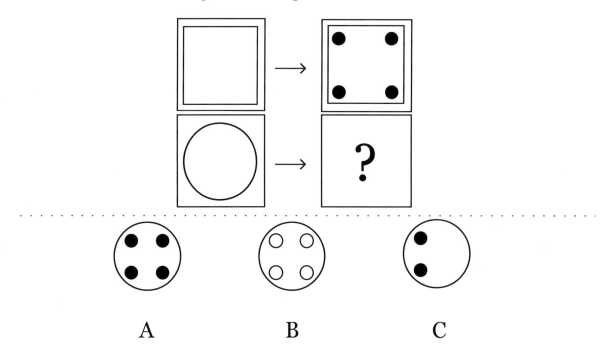

A   B   C

Correct Answer: A

Answer Explanation

In the top row, there are two figures that go together in a certain way. They go together in the sense that as the figure moves from left box to right box, it stays the same shape (a square) but adds four black circles inside.

Your child needs to find the figure among the answer options that fits best in the question mark box on the bottom row. The correct choice will have the same relationship with the figure on the bottom row that the figures in the top row have with each other.

Option B is incorrect because, although the figure is the same shape as the figure on the bottom row, the inside circles that are added are white.

Option C is incorrect because, although the figure is the same shape as the figure on the bottom row, only two black inside circles are added.

Option A is correct as the figure has the same shape (circle) as the figure on the bottom row and it has four black circles inside.

TEACHING TIPS

- Make sure your student knows key concepts that come up in these types of questions, including geometric concepts such as rotational symmetry, line symmetry, parts of a whole.

- If your student is finding these items difficult, encourage her to discover the pattern by isolating one element (e.g: outer shape, inner shape/s) and identify how it changes:
  → Ask: Is the color/shading of the element changing as it moves?
  → Ask: Is the element changing positions as it moves? Does it move up or down? Clockwise or counter-clockwise? Does it end up in the opposite (mirror) position?
  → Ask: Does the element disappear or increase in number as it moves along the row? Does it get bigger or smaller?

- Encourage your student to make a prediction for the missing object and compare the description with the answer choices.

Paper Folding

There are 14 Paper Folding questions in the CogAT® Level 8

SAMPLE QUESTION

The paper in the top row is folded and cut as shown. Which paper in the bottom row is the result when the paper is unfolded?

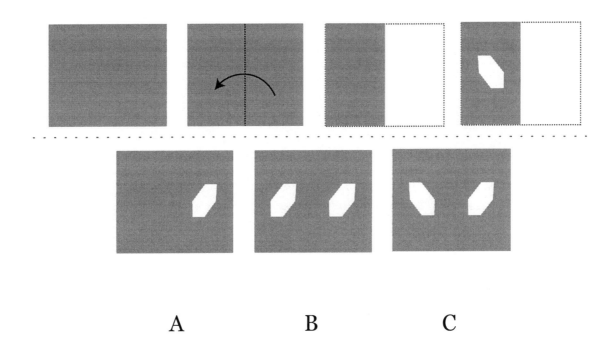

A   B   C

Correct Answer: C

Answer Explanation

In the top row, the paper is folded in half vertically. A shape is cut out of the folded paper.

Your child needs to choose which answer option shows how the paper will look when unfolded. The correct choice will be an unfolded paper with two shapes cut out of it. The shape on the right will mirror the shape on the left.

Option A is incorrect as it shows only one shape cut out from the paper.

Option B is incorrect as both shapes are placed in the same direction and are not mirror images of each other.

Option C is correct as the right shape reflects the left shape, like a mirror image.

TEACHING TIPS

* In addition to using the written practice questions, a good way to prepare for this unique and challenging question type is through hands-on practice with real paper. For example, you can show your student that if a paper is folded once and a hole is punched into it, she will see two holes on either side of the fold once the paper is unfolded.

CogAT® Quantitative Battery
Sample Questions & Teaching Tips

This battery includes three types of questions.

i.   Number Series
ii. Number Puzzles
iii. Number Analogies

If your child is going to go through the battery as if s/he were taking it under real testing conditions, then you should allow 45 minutes to complete this battery.

Otherwise, have your child answer each question in his or her own time, while you guide and give feedback as s/he progresses. Spend a few minutes reviewing the teaching tips for each section so you can help your student if he struggles with a question.

Before starting the battery, have your child try the sample questions in the next few pages.

Number Series

There are 18 Number Series questions in the CogAT® Level 8.

SAMPLE QUESTION

Which picture goes in the box with the question mark?

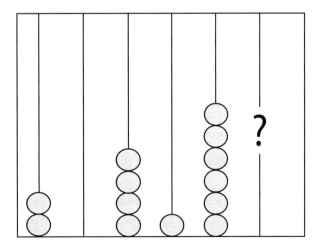
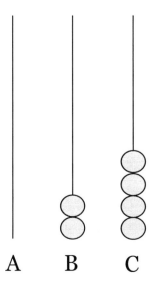

A   B   C

Correct Answer: B

Answer Explanation

The question shows an abacus with beads in a particular pattern.

Your child needs to figure out the pattern of the abacus beads and identify the answer choice which continues the pattern.

If your child looks from left to right, s/he can notice that the pattern of the beads is the following: The beads on the 1st, 3rd, and 5th rods increase by 2. The beads on the 2nd and 4th rods increase by 1. The pattern is 2, 0, 4, 1, 6, 2. The answer is therefore B (2 beads).

TEACHING TIPS

- Because your child may not have much formal academic experience with this question type, it is important to practice working with many of these questions before the test.

- It may be helpful to model how to approach the questions for your child. Read the question aloud, and then do a "think-aloud," talking through your thought process as you solve the problem.

- You can also find workbooks or games related to number patterns and sequences to help your child further his or her understanding of these concepts in an engaging manner.

Number Puzzles

There are 14 Number Puzzles questions in the CogAT® Level 8

SAMPLE QUESTION

Which picture goes in the box with the question mark?

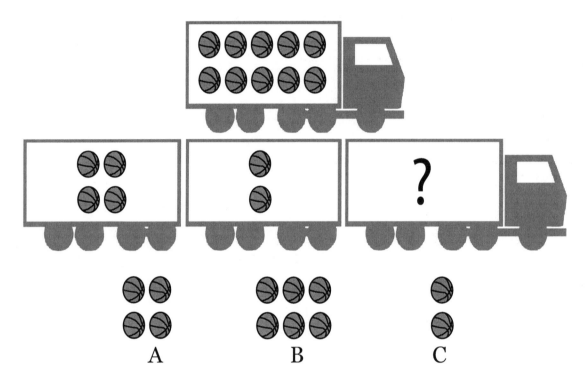

A   B   C

Correct answer: A

Answer Explanation

In the train on the top row, there are 10 balls. In the train on the bottom row, there are four balls in one compartment and two balls in another.

Your child needs to figure out how many balls are needed in the compartment with the question mark so that both trains (top and bottom row), have the same amount of balls.

We can see that four balls are needed in order to make a total of 10 balls in the train on the bottom row, because 4 balls from one compartment plus 2 balls from the other compartment results in a total of 6 balls (4+2=6), and we need four more balls in the train to have 10 balls in total (6+4=10). The only answer that shows 4 balls is option A.

TEACHING TIPS

- This question type requires your child to solve basic math equations, so practice with numbers and problem solving is essential.

- Make sure your child understands the meaning of "equal," since the object is to supply the missing piece of information that will make two provided equations (objects in trains) equal to one another

- Try using hands-on materials (like blocks, beads or marbles) to help a student become confident with adding and subtracting. For example, you might give your student two marbles and then ask her to "add" three more marbles to the pile. Then, ask her to count how many marbles she now has. This works with subtraction, too.

- You can also teach your child to approach the question by "plugging in" the answer choices and solving to see if the result is equal to the other equation in the question.

Number Analogies

There are 18 Number Analogies questions in the CogAT® Level 8

SAMPLE QUESTION

Which image best fits in the box with the question mark?

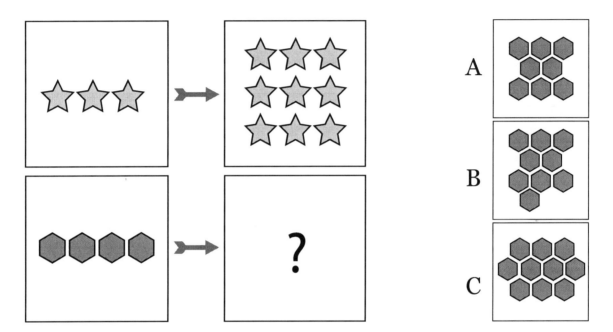

Correct answer: C

Answer Explanation

In the top row, there are two pictures that go together. As we move from the left picture to the picture on the right, the 3 stars become 9 stars. This means that 6 stars have been added to the 3 stars to make 9 stars.

Your child needs to find the picture among the answer options that best fits in the question mark box. The correct choice has the same relationship with the picture on the left on the bottom row as the two pictures in the top row have with each other.

The bottom row picture shows 4 hexagons. To match the relationship in the top row, your child needs to add 6 hexagons to the 4 hexagons in the first box to give a total of 10 hexagons.

Option C is therefore correct as the picture shows 10 hexagons.

TEACHING TIPS

- Your child is probably not accustomed to completing number matrices, so it is important to frequently expose him to this question type in order to build confidence and familiarity.

- Make sure your child has an understanding/recognition of the following relationships:

  → Part/whole (or reverse: whole/part)

  → Changes in quantity

  → Changes in size.

- Consider modeling how to approach solving a number matrix by "thinking aloud" as you work through a question with your child.

- Work with your child on basic mathematical concepts (see teaching tips for Number Puzzles).

CogAT® Level 8
Practice Test

CogAT®
Verbal Battery

Sentence Completion

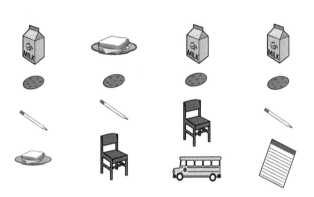

Picture Classifications

Picture Analogies

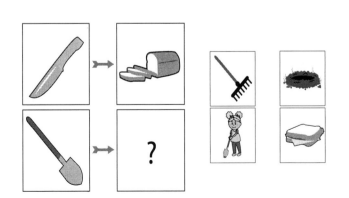

CogAT® Level 8 Test Prep Book

Gifted & Talented Test Prep Team

Sentence Completion
Practice Questions

Which picture shows a black triangle under a black heart and a white star?

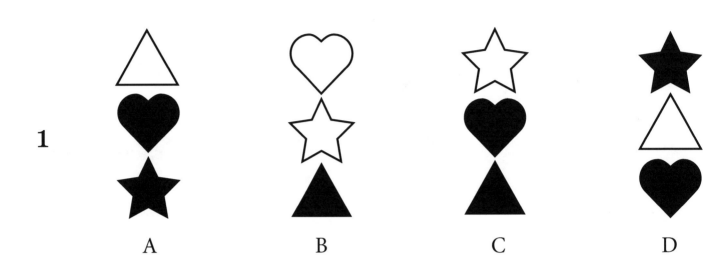

1

| A | B | C | D |

When Jessie gets home from school, she drinks milk, eats a cookie, and writes a note. Which picture show all the things Jessie uses when she gets home?

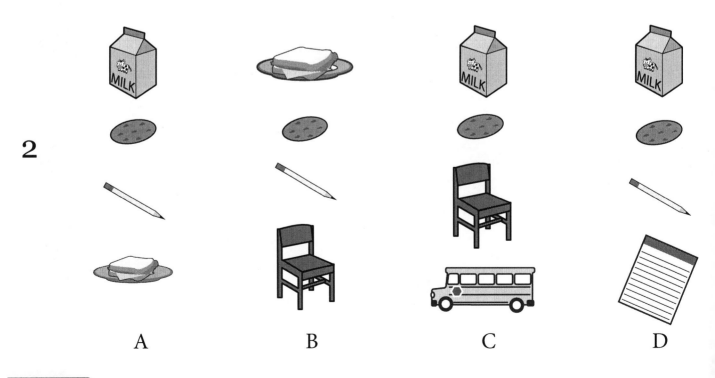

2

| A | B | C | D |

James eats 3 strawberries and a carrot every day. His sister eats fewer strawberries, but also a banana every day. She does not eat vegetables. Which picture shows what James' sister eats every day.

3

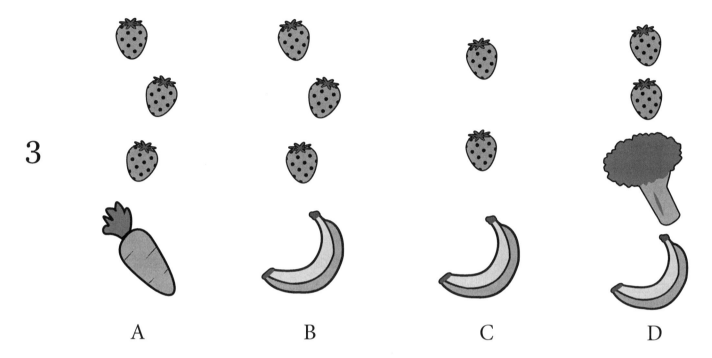

A   B   C   D

Lauren went to the store to buy an apple, an orange, a pear, and a banana. She forgot to buy a pear. Which picture shows what Lauren bought at the store?

4

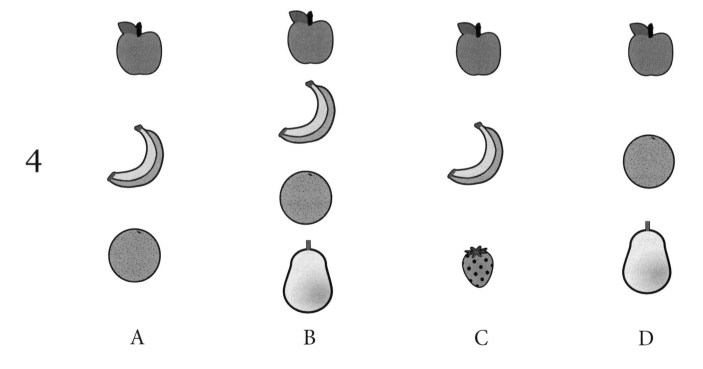

A   B   C   D

Sentence Completion

Greg is wearing a black shirt, black shoes, and white shorts. Jake's outfit is the opposite of Greg's. Which picture shows what Jake is wearing?

5

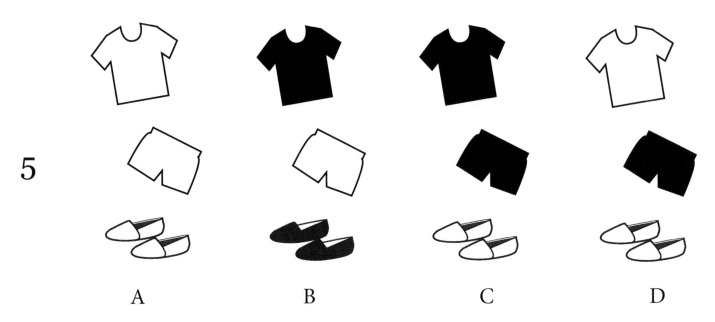

A   B   C   D

Which picture shows a square inside of a heart in between a black star and a white star?

6

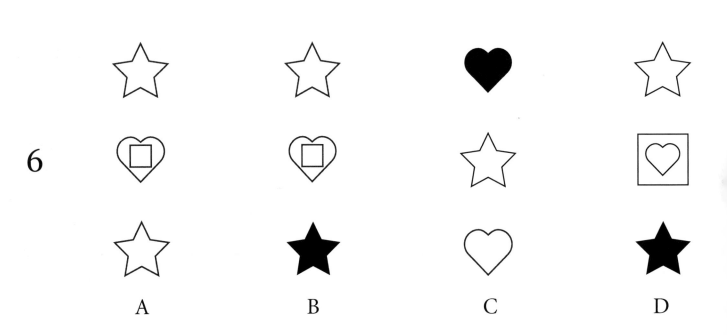

A   B   C   D

Sentence Completion

Which picture shows this: There is a black circle between a black heart and white rectangle?

7

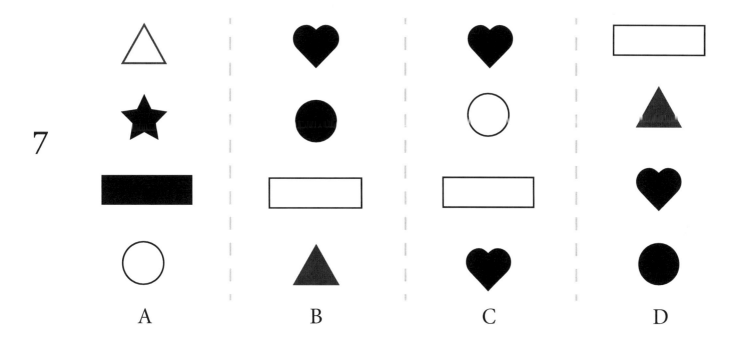

A   B   C   D

Isla and Melodie both play instruments. Isla plays instruments with strings. Melodie plays the same instruments as Isla, but she also plays the flute. Which picture shows what Melodie plays?

8

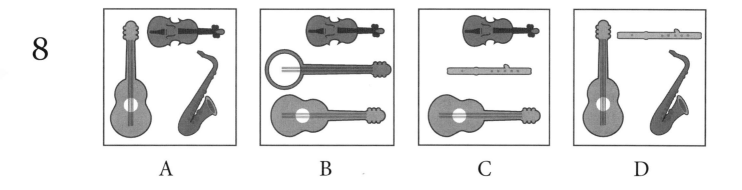

A   B   C   D

Sentence Completion

Jerry is late for his appointment at the doctor. He wants to get to the doctor's office quickly. Which picture shows what he uses to get to the doctor's office?

9

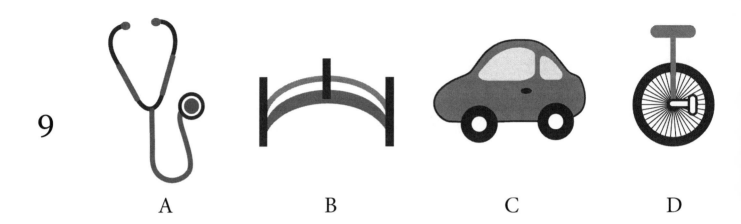

A   B   C   D

Which picture shows the cat between the horse and the snake? The bee is above the snake and the horse is below the cat

10

A   B   C   D

Sentence Completion

To help her make dinner, Ariana used an oven, a saucepan, and a large bowl. Mark the picture which shows the kitchen equipment Ariana did not use.

11

    A   B   C   D

Alfred went to the forest with his family. On the trail, he saw a reptile, two mammals, and an insect. Which picture shows the animals that Alfred saw.

12

    A   B   C   D

Sentence Completion

Betsy is a pharmacist. Which picture shows what Betsy might use when she is working?

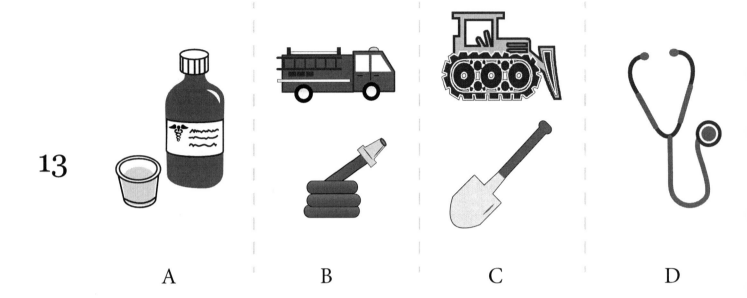

13

A   B   C   D

Which of these items might you find in a hardware store?

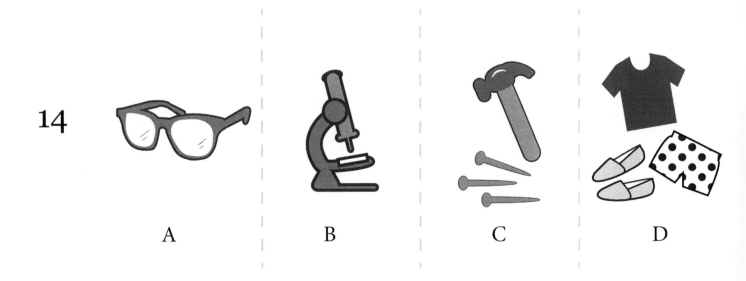

14

A   B   C   D

Which picture shows an animal that is a predator?

15

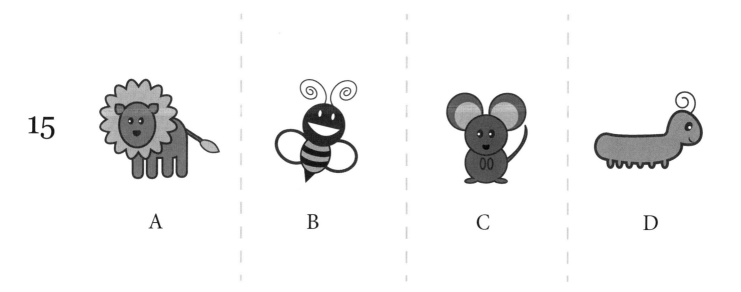

A   B   C   D

Which picture shows a vacant room?

16

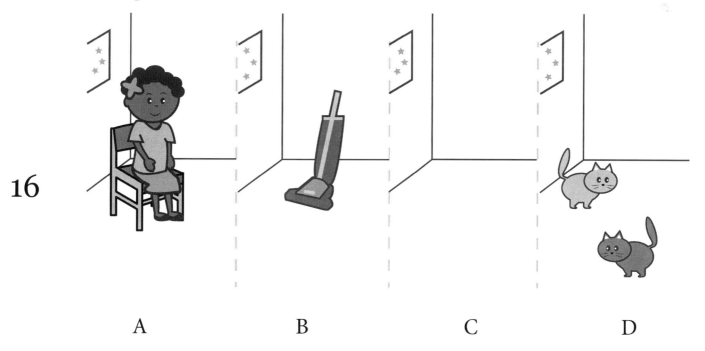

A   B   C   D

Sentence Completion

Which picture shows a boy descending a steep hill?

17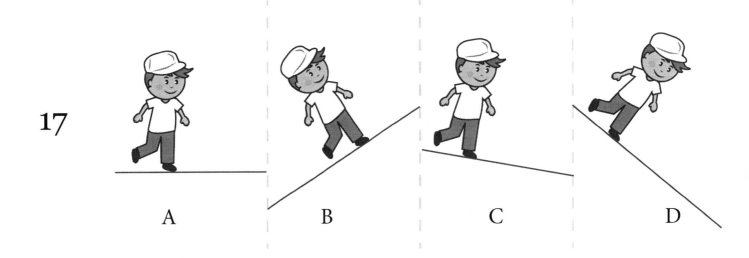

Which picture would you choose to represent the word "vain"?

18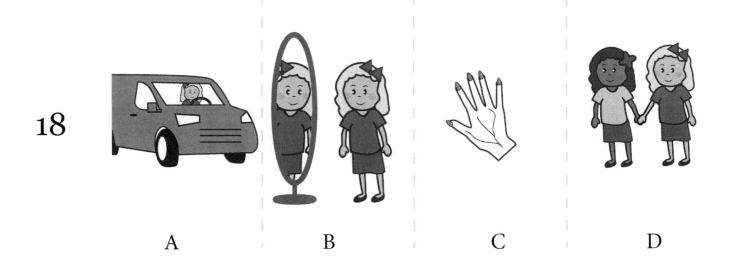

CogAT® Level 8 Test Prep Book   Gifted & Talented Test Prep Team

Picture Classifications
Practice Questions

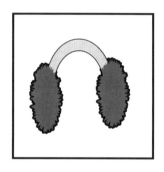 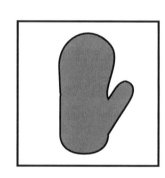 

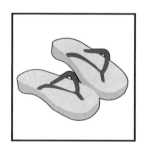  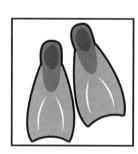

Picture Classifications

Look at the pictures in the boxes in the top row. These pictures go together in a certain way. Which picture in the bottom row goes with the pictures in the top row?

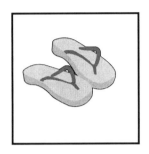 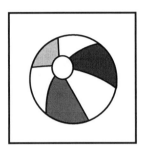 

1

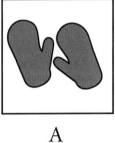  (C) (D)

    A   B   C   D

Look at the pictures in the boxes in the top row. These pictures go together in a certain way. Which picture in the bottom row goes with the pictures in the top row?

2

    A   B   C   D

Picture Classifications

Look at the pictures in the boxes in the top row. These pictures go together in a certain way. Which picture in the bottom row goes with the pictures in the top row?

3

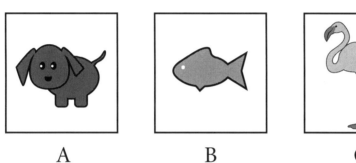

A   B   C   D

Look at the pictures in the boxes in the top row. These pictures go together in a certain way. Which picture in the bottom row goes with the pictures in the top row?

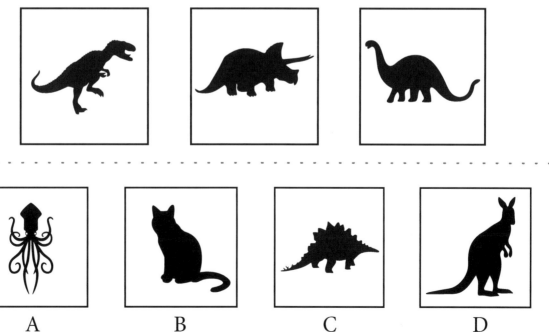

4

A   B   C   D

Picture Classifications

Look at the pictures in the boxes in the top row. These pictures go together in a certain way. Which picture in the bottom row goes with the pictures in the top row?

5

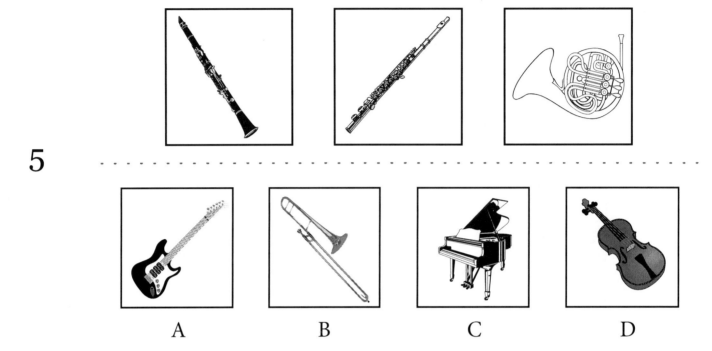

A   B   C   D

Look at the pictures in the boxes in the top row. These pictures go together in a certain way. Which picture in the bottom row goes with the pictures in the top row?

6

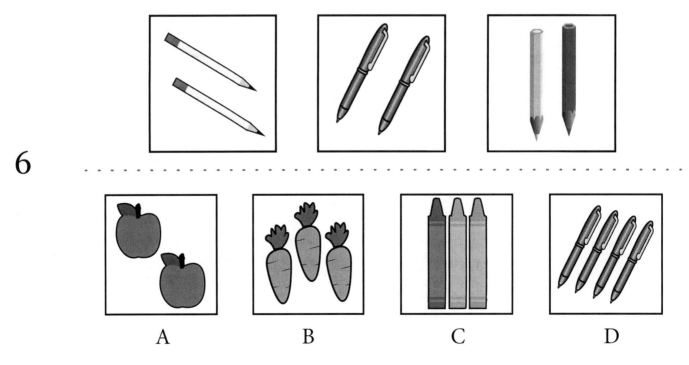

A   B   C   D

Picture Classifications

Look at the pictures in the boxes in the top row. These pictures go together in a certain way. Which picture in the bottom row goes with the pictures in the top row?

 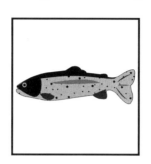 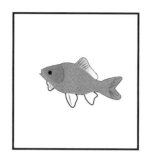

7

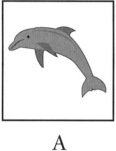   

A　　　　　　B　　　　　　C　　　　　　D

Look at the pictures in the boxes in the top row. These pictures go together in a certain way. Which picture in the bottom row goes with the pictures in the top row?

8

A　　　　　　B　　　　　　C　　　　　　D

Picture Classifications

Look at the pictures in the boxes in the top row. These pictures go together in a certain way. Which picture in the bottom row goes with the pictures in the top row?

9

A   B   C   D

Look at the pictures in the boxes in the top row. These pictures go together in a certain way. Which picture in the bottom row goes with the pictures in the top row?

 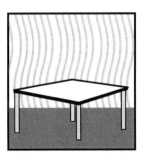 

10

A   B   C   D

Look at the pictures in the boxes in the top row. These pictures go together in a certain way. Which picture in the bottom row goes with the pictures in the top row?

 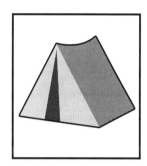 

11

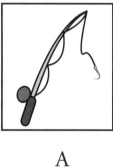

A   B   C   D

Look at the pictures in the boxes in the top row. These pictures go together in a certain way. Which picture in the bottom row goes with the pictures in the top row?

12

A   B   C   D

Picture Classifications

Look at the pictures in the boxes in the top row. These pictures go together in a certain way. Which picture in the bottom row goes with the pictures in the top row?

13

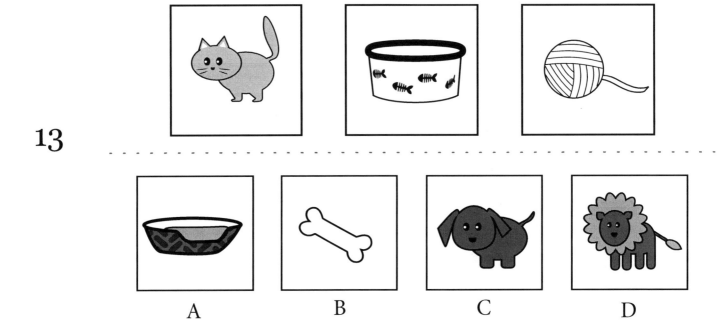

A   B   C   D

Look at the pictures in the boxes in the top row. These pictures go together in a certain way. Which picture in the bottom row goes with the pictures in the top row?

14

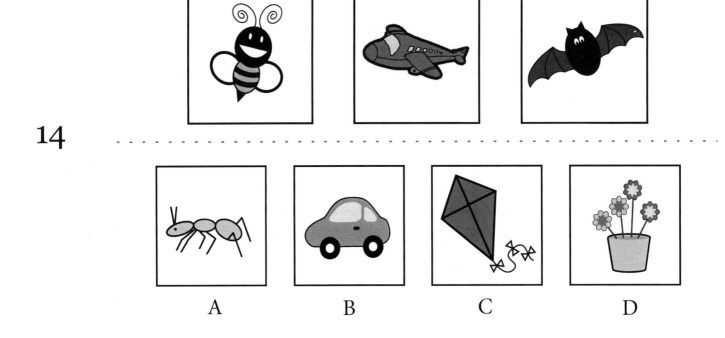

A   B   C   D

Picture Classifications

Look at the pictures in the boxes in the top row. These pictures go together in a certain way. Which picture in the bottom row goes with the pictures in the top row?

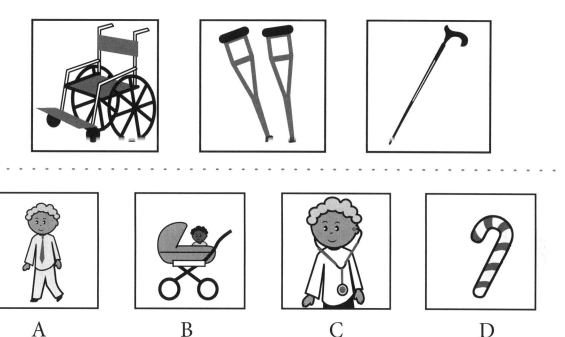

15

    A   B   C   D

Look at the pictures in the boxes in the top row. These pictures go together in a certain way. Which picture in the bottom row goes with the pictures in the top row?

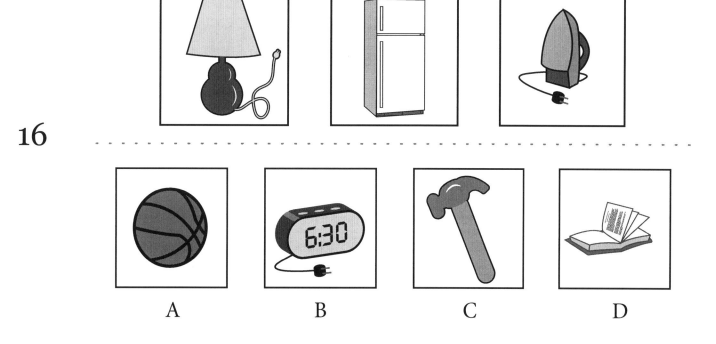

16

    A   B   C   D

Picture Classifications

Look at the pictures in the boxes in the top row. These pictures go together in a certain way. Which picture in the bottom row goes with the pictures in the top row?

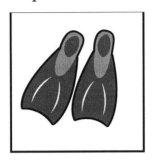  

17

A   B   C   D

Look at the pictures in the boxes in the top row. These pictures go together in a certain way. Which picture in the bottom row goes with the pictures in the top row?

18

 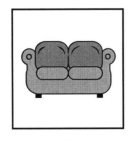  

A   B   C   D

Picture Analogies
Practice Questions

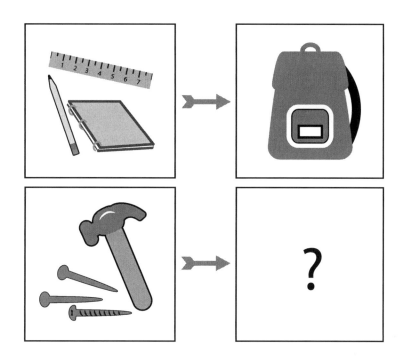

Which image best fits in the box with the question mark?

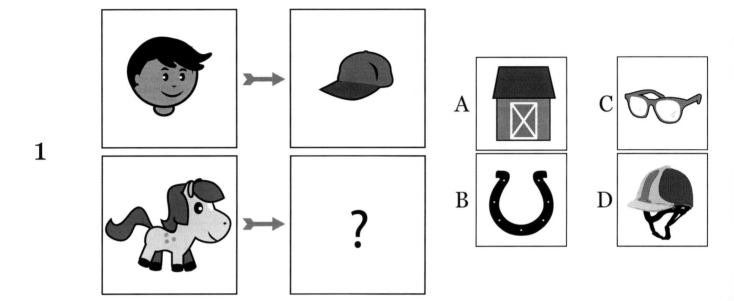

Which image best fits in the box with the question mark?

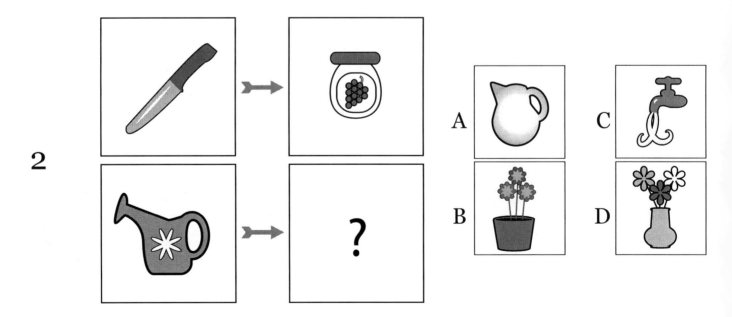

Picture Analogies

Which image best fits in the box with the question mark?

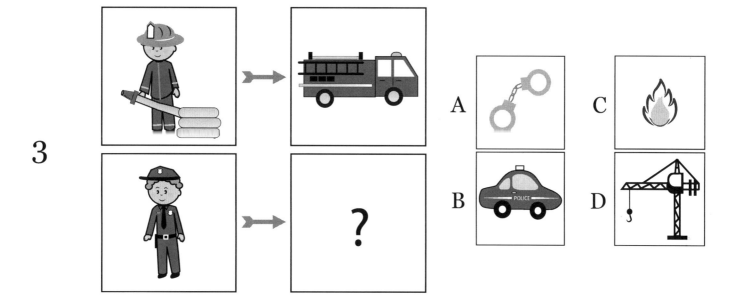

Which image best fits in the box with the question mark?

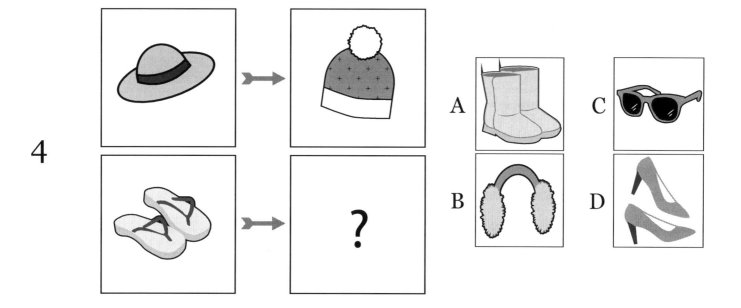

Picture Analogies

Which image best fits in the box with the question mark?

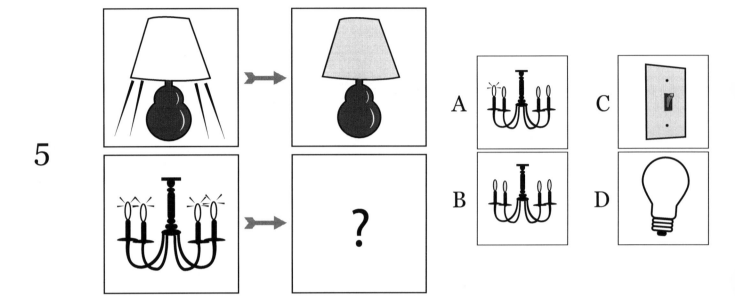

Which image best fits in the box with the question mark?

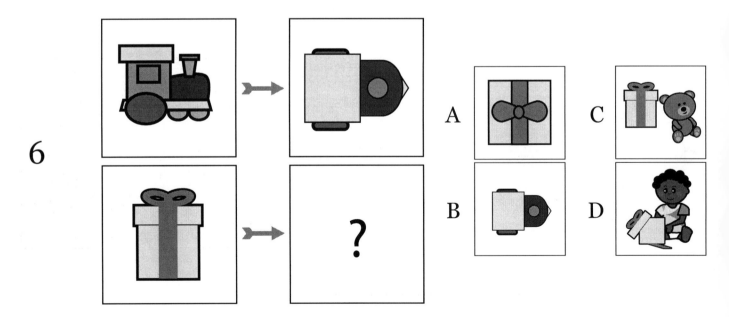

Picture Analogies

Which image best fits in the box with the question mark?

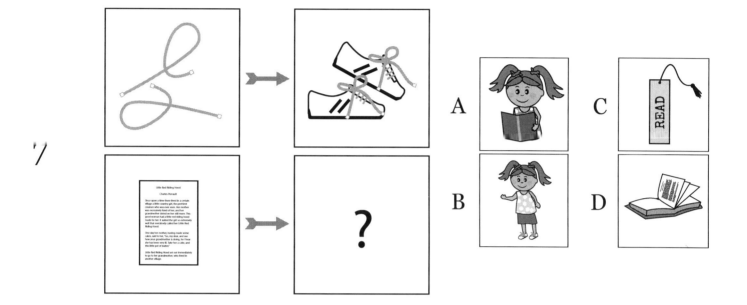

Which image best fits in the box with the question mark?

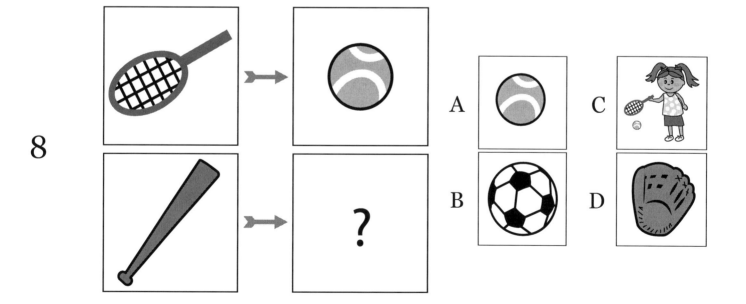

Picture Analogies

Which image best fits in the box with the question mark?

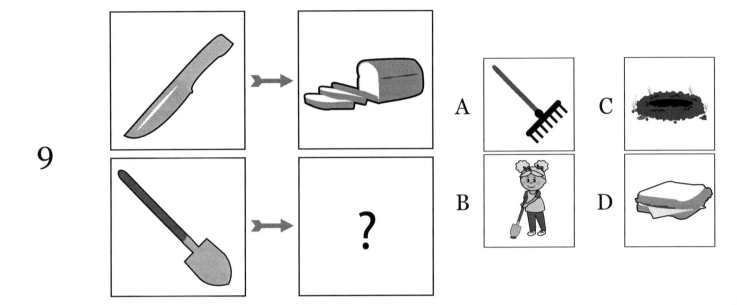

Which image best fits in the box with the question mark?

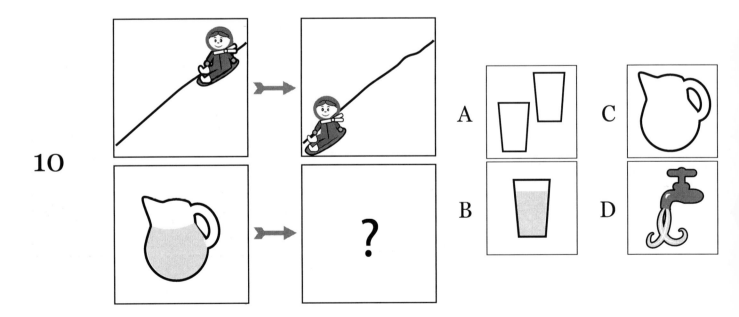

CogAT® Level 8 Test Prep Book   Gifted & Talented Test Prep Team

Which image best fits in the box with the question mark?

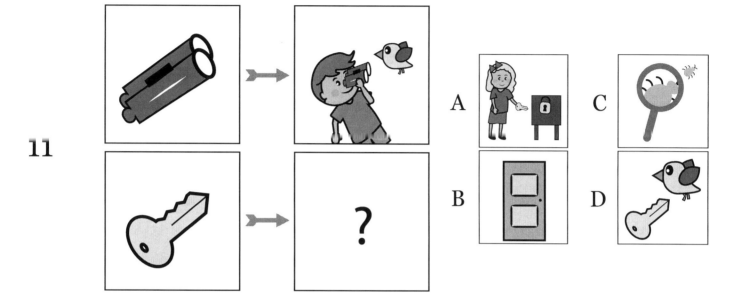

11

Which image best fits in the box with the question mark?

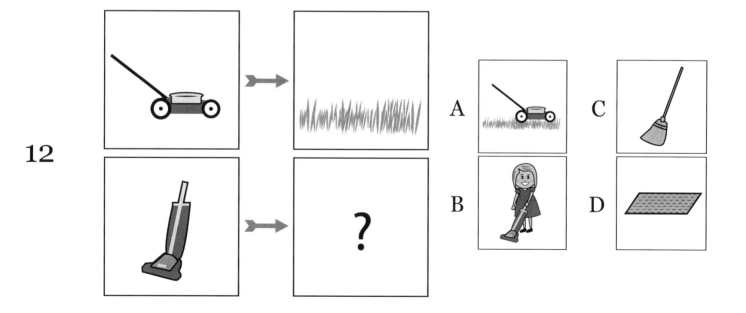

12

Picture Analogies

Which image best fits in the box with the question mark?

13

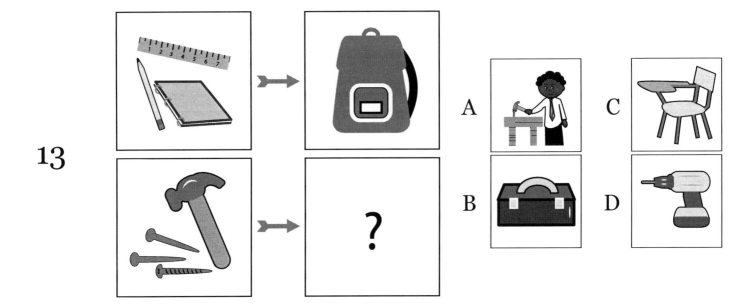

Which image best fits in the box with the question mark?

14

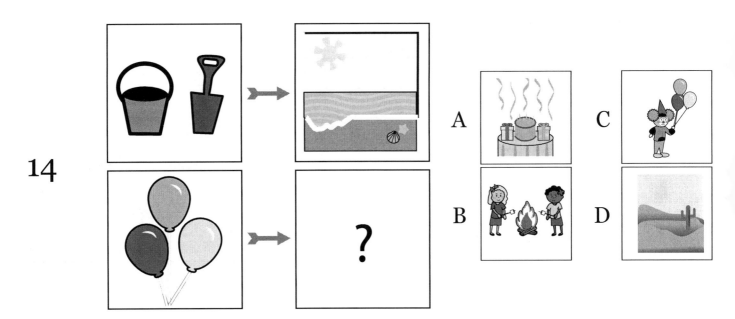

Picture Analogies

Which image best fits in the box with the question mark?

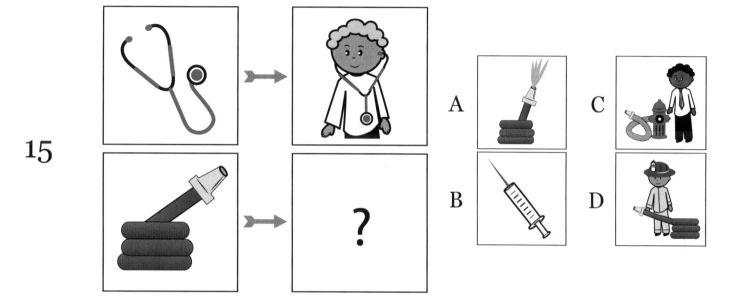

Which image best fits in the box with the question mark?

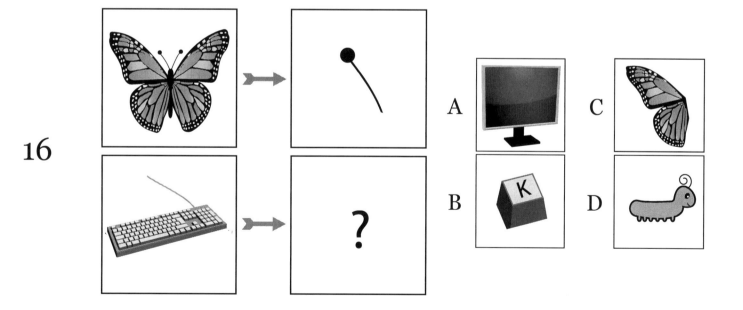

Picture Analogies

Which image best fits in the box with the question mark?

17

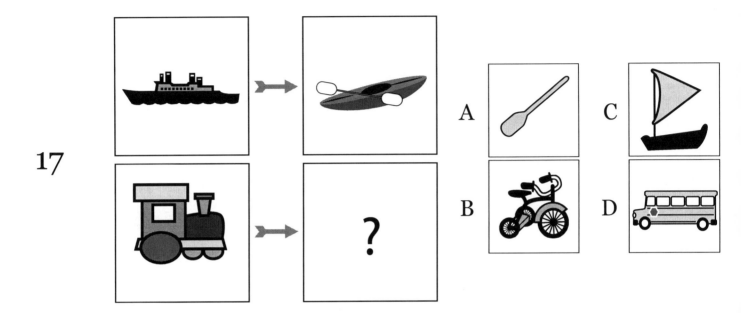

Which image best fits in the box with the question mark?

18

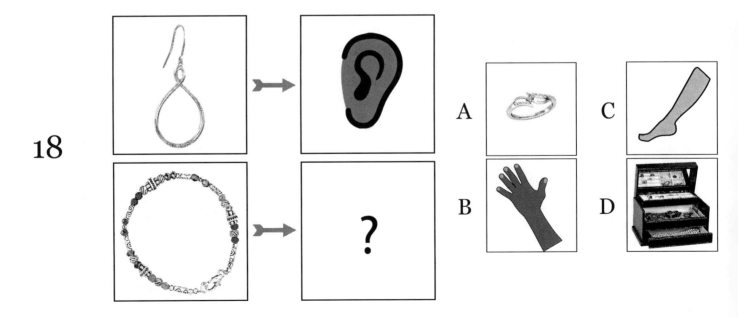

Gifted & Talented Test Prep Team

CogAT®
Nonverbal Battery

Figure Matrices

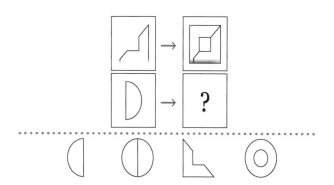

Figure Classification

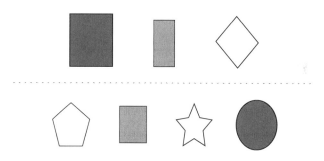

Paper Folding

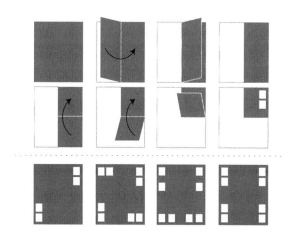

Figure Matrices
Practice Questions

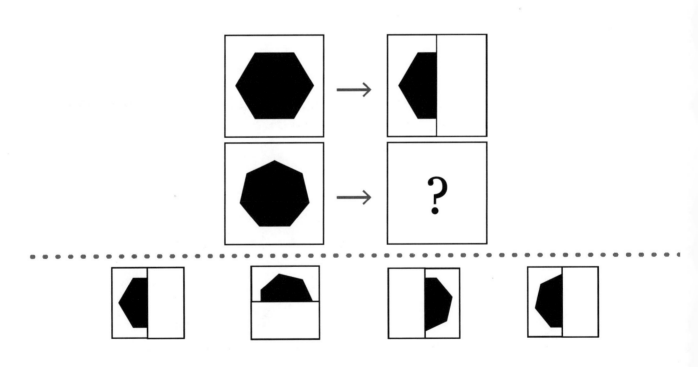

Figure Matrices

Look at the shapes in the boxes on top. These shapes go together in a certain way. Which shape belongs where the question mark is?

1

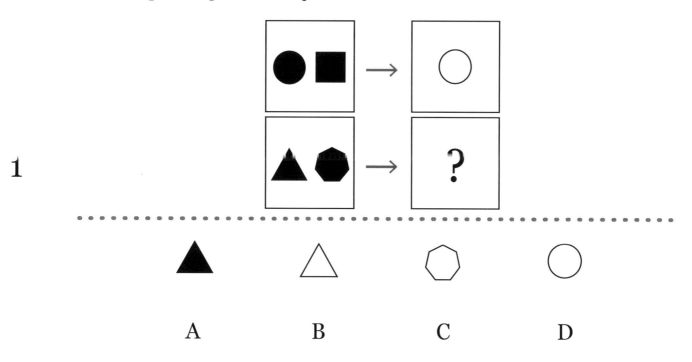

A B C D

Look at the shapes in the boxes on top. These shapes go together in a certain way. Which shape belongs where the question mark is?

2

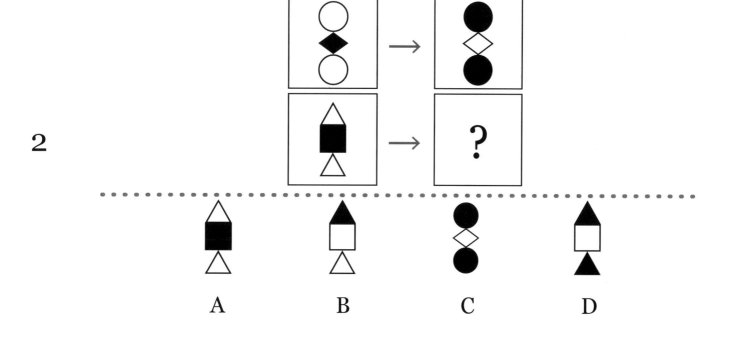

A B C D

Look at the shapes in the boxes on top. These shapes go together in a certain way. Which shape belongs where the question mark is?

3

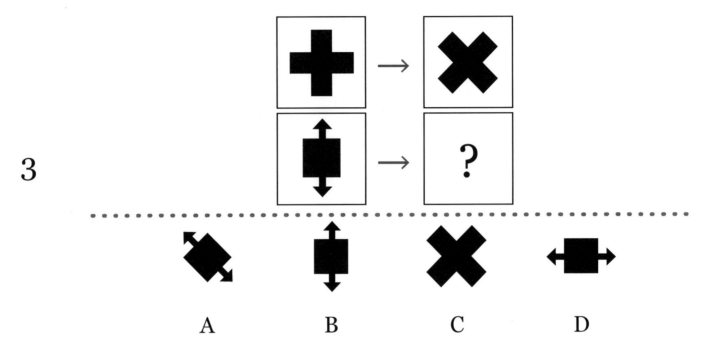

A   B   C   D

Look at the shapes in the boxes on top. These shapes go together in a certain way. Which shape belongs where the question mark is?

4

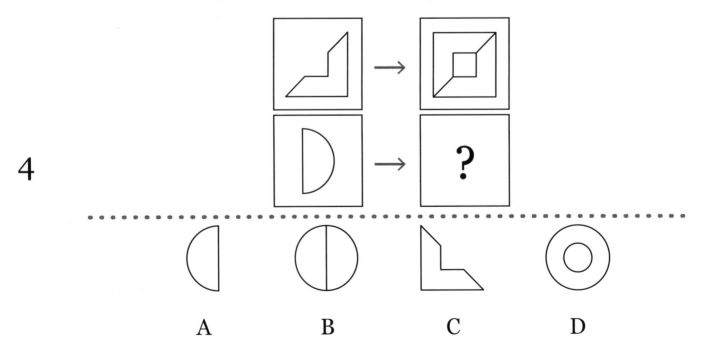

A   B   C   D

Look at the shapes in the boxes on top. These shapes go together in a certain way. Which shape belongs where the question mark is?

5

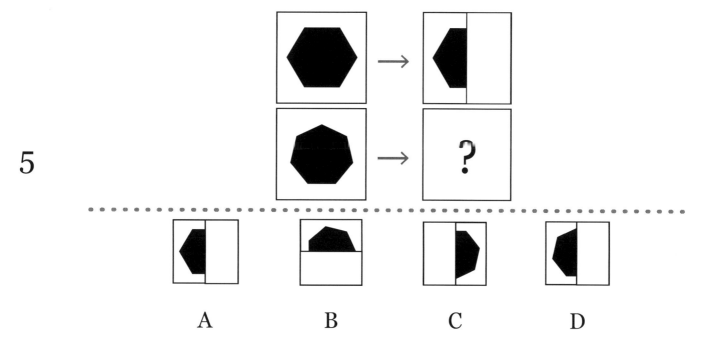

A   B   C   D

Look at the shapes in the boxes on top. These shapes go together in a certain way. Which shape belongs where the question mark is?

6

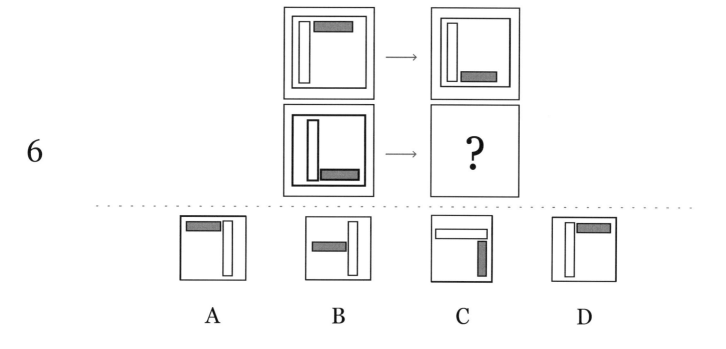

A   B   C   D

Figure Matrices

Look at the shapes in the boxes on top. These shapes go together in a certain way. Which shape belongs where the question mark is?

7

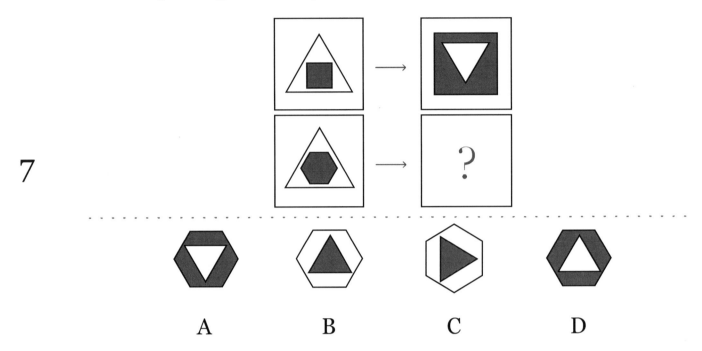

| A | B | C | D |

Look at the shapes in the boxes on top. These shapes go together in a certain way. Which shape belongs where the question mark is?

8

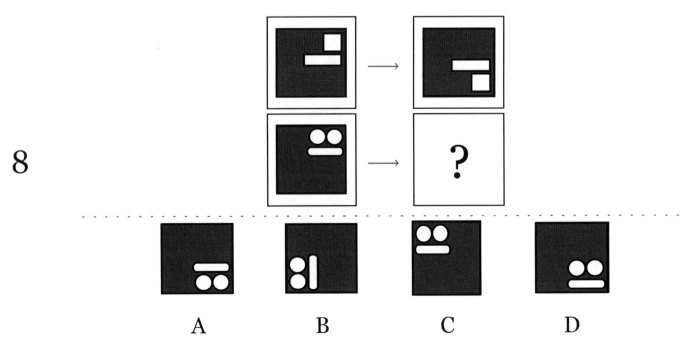

| A | B | C | D |

Figure Matrices

Look at the shapes in the boxes on top. These shapes go together in a certain way. Which shape belongs where the question mark is?

9

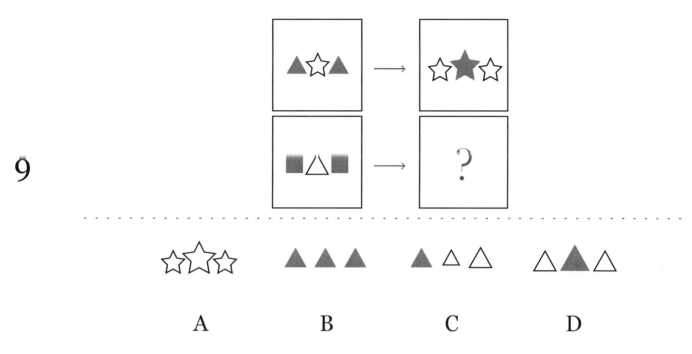

A   B   C   D

Look at the shapes in the boxes on top. These shapes go together in a certain way. Which shape belongs where the question mark is?

10

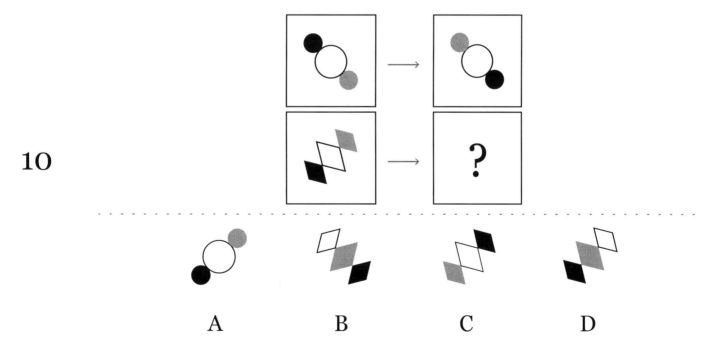

A   B   C   D

Figure Matrices

Look at the shapes in the boxes on top. These shapes go together in a certain way. Which shape belongs where the question mark is?

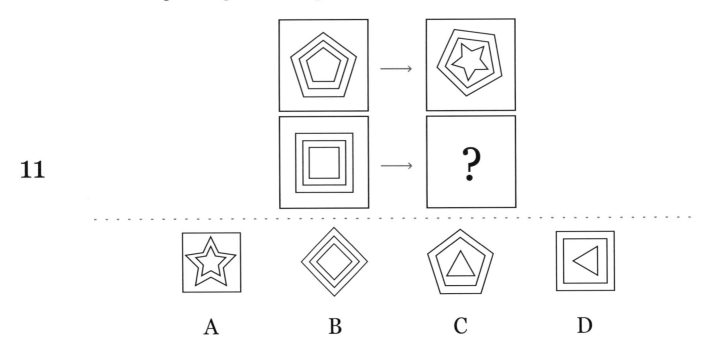

11

A   B   C   D

Look at the shapes in the boxes on top. These shapes go together in a certain way. Which shape belongs where the question mark is?

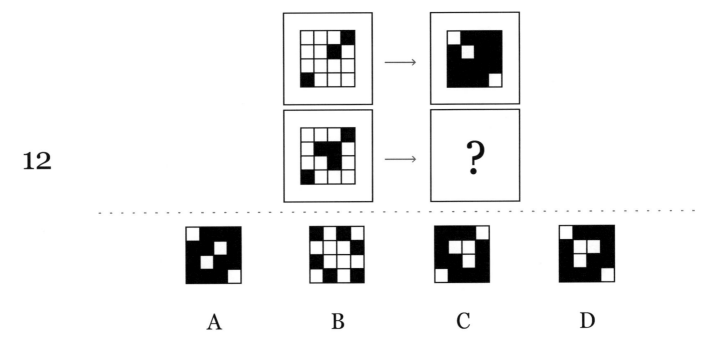

12

A   B   C   D

CogAT® Level 8 Test Prep Book   Gifted & Talented Test Prep Team

Look at the shapes in the boxes on top. These shapes go together in a certain way. Which shape belongs where the question mark is?

13

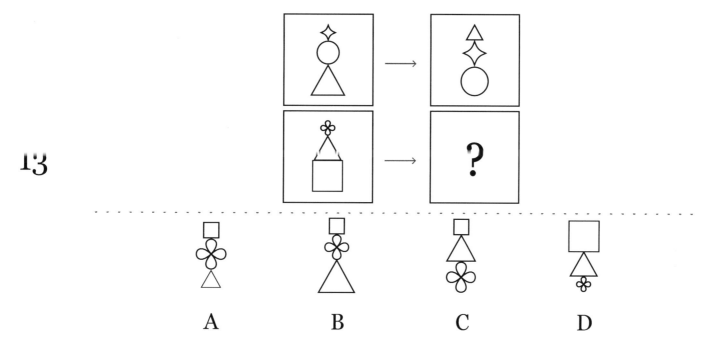

| A | B | C | D |

Look at the shapes in the boxes on top. These shapes go together in a certain way. Which shape belongs where the question mark is?

14

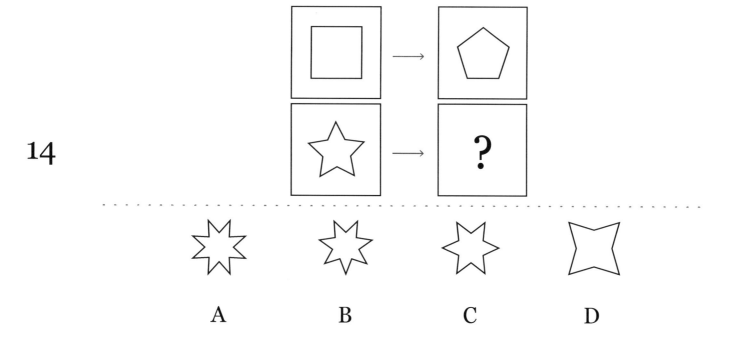

| A | B | C | D |

Look at the shapes in the boxes on top. These shapes go together in a certain way. Which shape belongs where the question mark is?

15

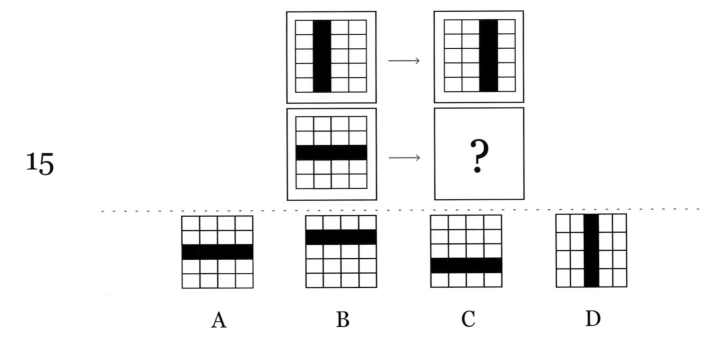

A   B   C   D

Look at the shapes in the boxes on top. These shapes go together in a certain way. Which shape belongs where the question mark is?

16

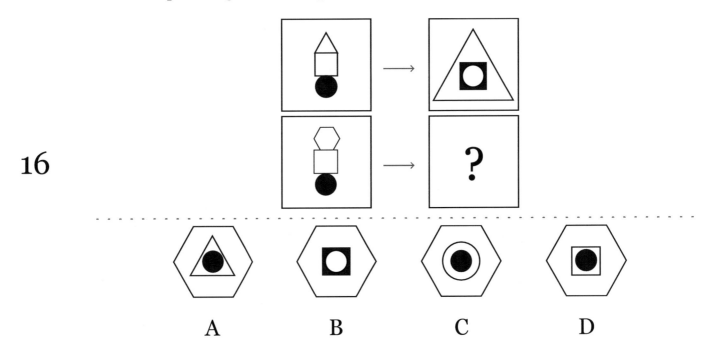

A   B   C   D

Look at the shapes in the boxes on top. These shapes go together in a certain way. Which shape belongs where the question mark is?

17

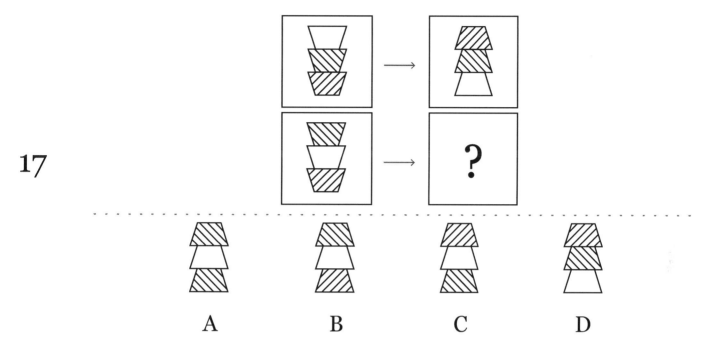

A   B   C   D

Look at the shapes in the boxes on top. These shapes go together in a certain way. Which shape belongs where the question mark is?

18

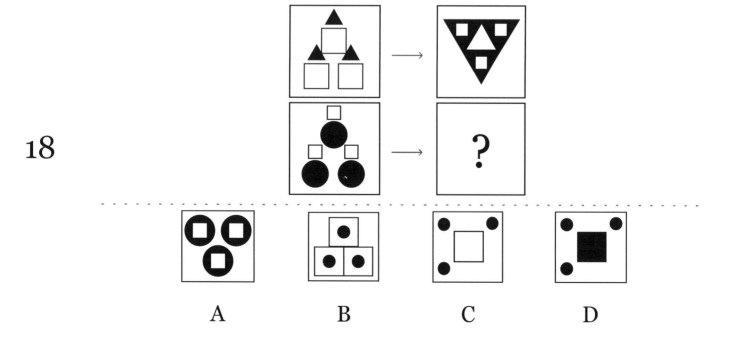

A   B   C   D

Figure Classifications
Practice Questions

  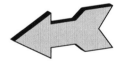

  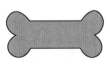

Figure Classifications

Look at the shapes in the top row. These shapes go together in a certain way. Which shape in the bottom row belongs with the shapes in the top row?

1

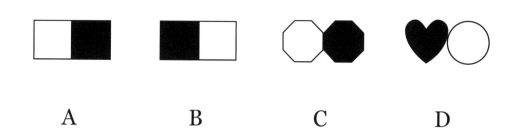

A   B   C   D

Look at the shapes in the top row. These shapes go together in a certain way. Which shape in the bottom row belongs with the shapes in the top row?

2

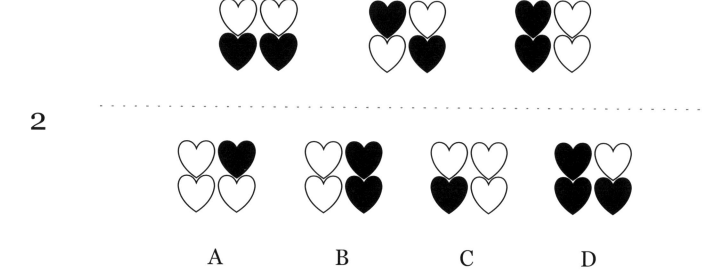

A   B   C   D

Figure Classifications

Look at the shapes in the top row. These shapes go together in a certain way. Which shape in the bottom row belongs with the shapes in the top row?

3

    A   B   C   D

Look at the shapes in the top row. These shapes go together in a certain way. Which shape in the bottom row belongs with the shapes in the top row?

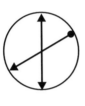 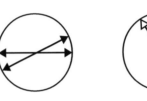

4

    A   B   C   D

Figure Classifications

Look at the shapes in the top row. These shapes go together in a certain way. Which shape in the bottom row belongs with the shapes in the top row?

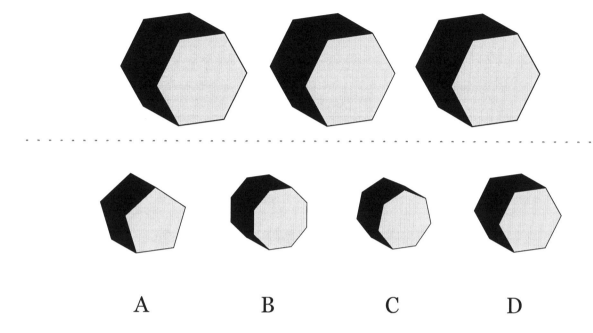

5

    A   B   C   D

Look at the shapes in the top row. These shapes go together in a certain way. Which shape in the bottom row belongs with the shapes in the top row?

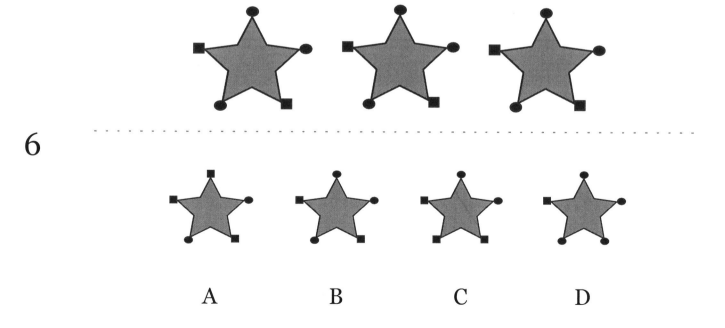

6

    A   B   C   D

Figure Classifications

Look at the shapes in the top row. These shapes go together in a certain way. Which shape in the bottom row belongs with the shapes in the top row?

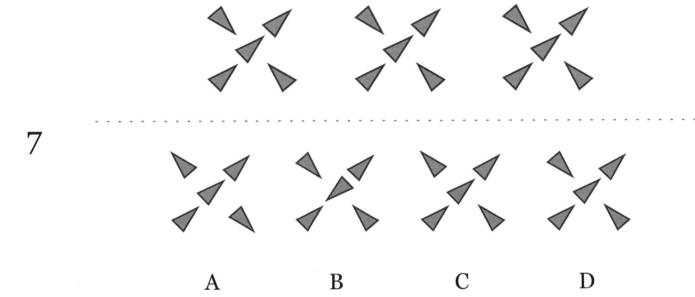

7

A   B   C   D

Look at the shapes in the top row. These shapes go together in a certain way. Which shape in the bottom row belongs with the shapes in the top row?

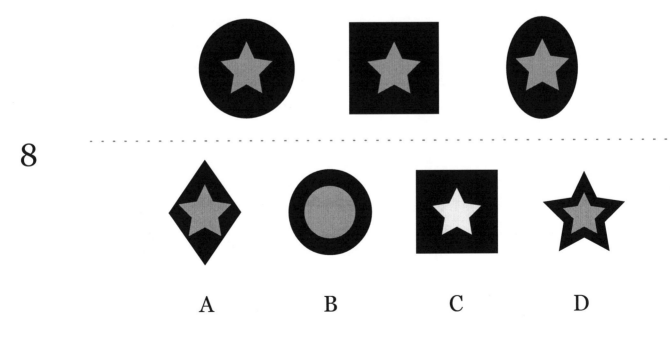

8

A   B   C   D

Figure Classifications

Look at the shapes in the top row. These shapes go together in a certain way. Which shape in the bottom row belongs with the shapes in the top row?

9

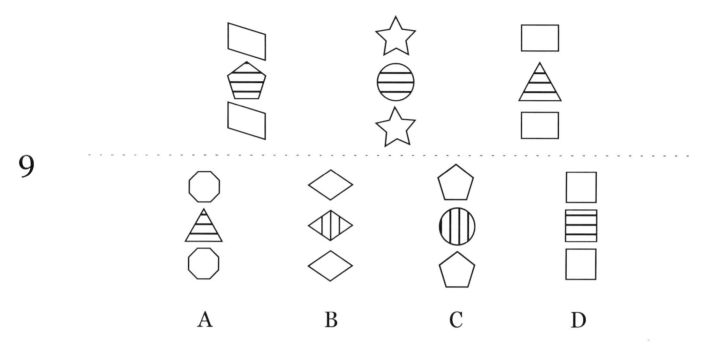

A   B   C   D

Look at the shapes in the top row. These shapes go together in a certain way. Which shape in the bottom row belongs with the shapes in the top row?

10

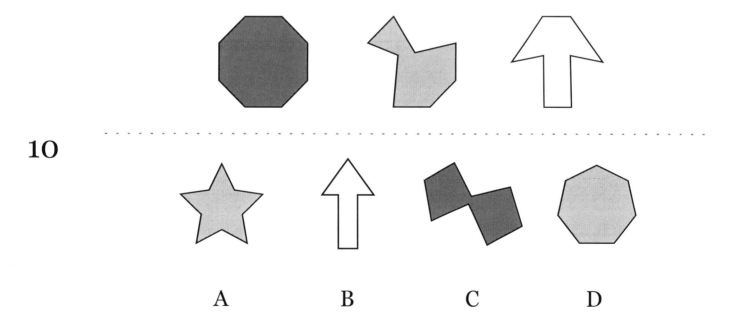

A   B   C   D

Look at the shapes in the top row. These shapes go together in a certain way. Which shape in the bottom row belongs with the shapes in the top row?

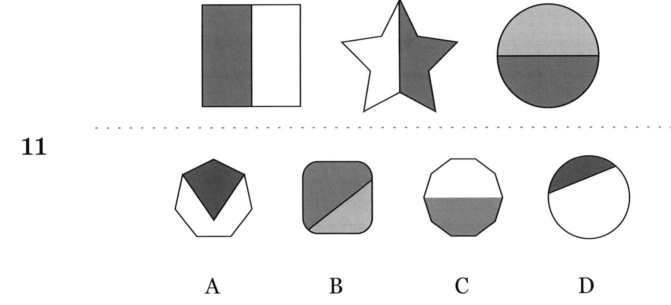

11

A   B   C   D

Look at the shapes in the top row. These shapes go together in a certain way. Which shape in the bottom row belongs with the shapes in the top row?

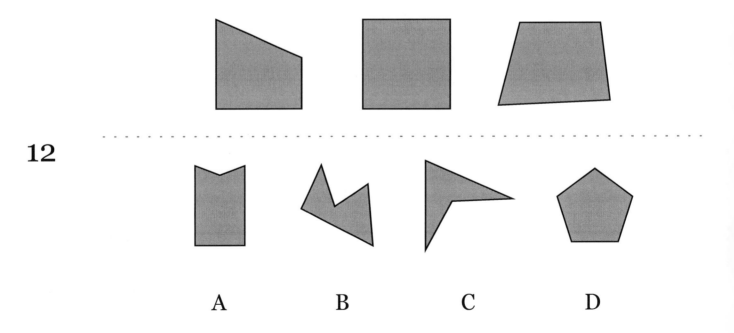

12

A   B   C   D

Look at the shapes in the top row. These shapes go together in a certain way. Which shape in the bottom row belongs with the shapes in the top row?

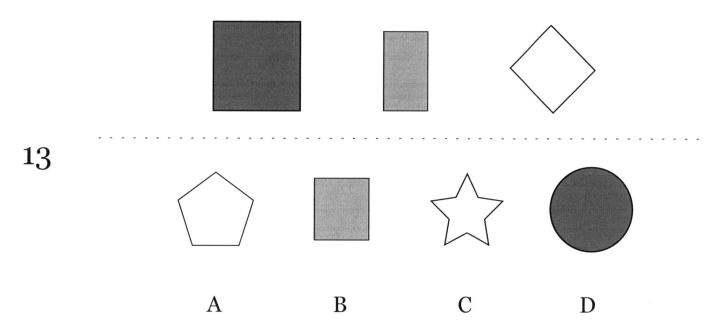

13

| A | B | C | D |

Look at the shapes in the top row. These shapes go together in a certain way. Which shape in the bottom row belongs with the shapes in the top row?

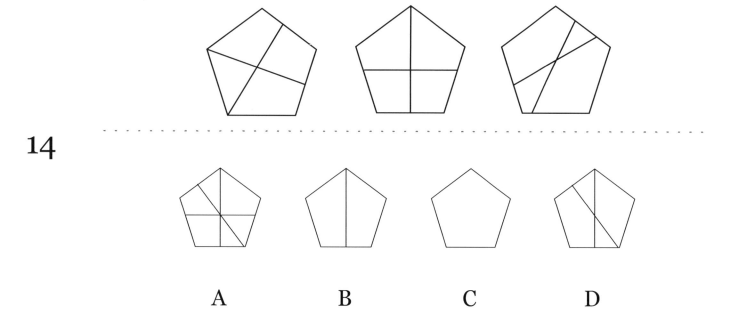

14

| A | B | C | D |

Figure Classifications

Look at the shapes in the top row. These shapes go together in a certain way. Which shape in the bottom row belongs with the shapes in the top row?

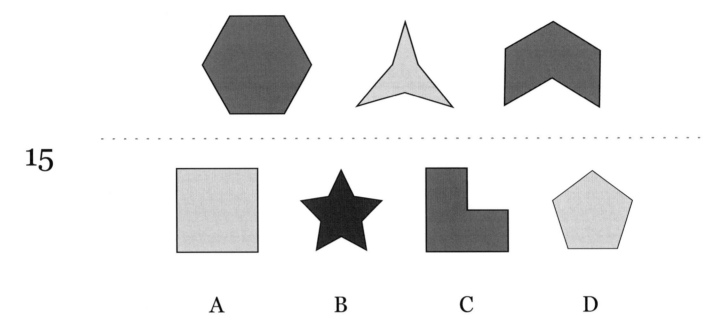

15

Look at the shapes in the top row. These shapes go together in a certain way. Which shape in the bottom row belongs with the shapes in the top row?

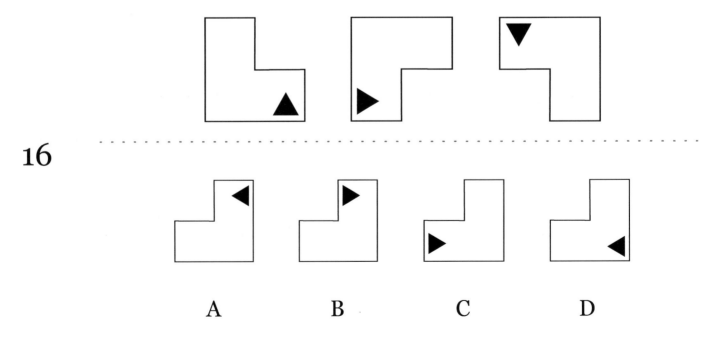

16

Look at the shapes in the top row. These shapes go together in a certain way. Which shape in the bottom row belongs with the shapes in the top row?

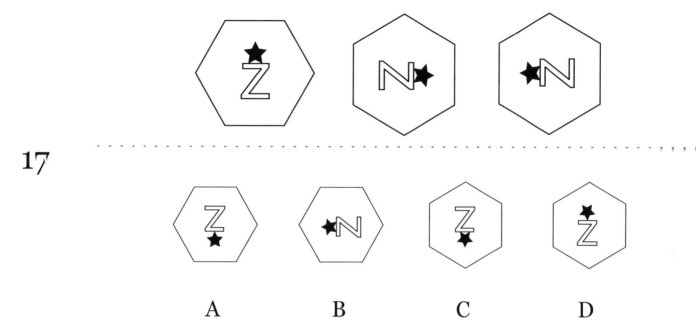

17

A   B   C   D

Look at the shapes in the top row. These shapes go together in a certain way. Which shape in the bottom row belongs with the shapes in the top row?

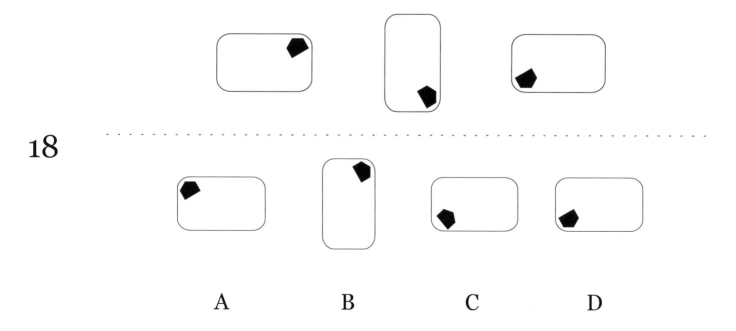

18

A   B   C   D

Paper Folding
Practice Questions

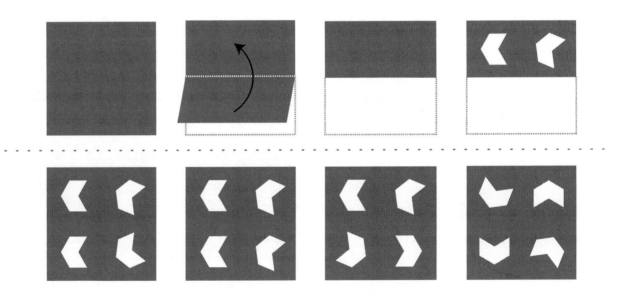

Paper Folding

The paper in the top row is folded and cut as shown. Which paper in the bottom row is the result when the paper is unfolded?

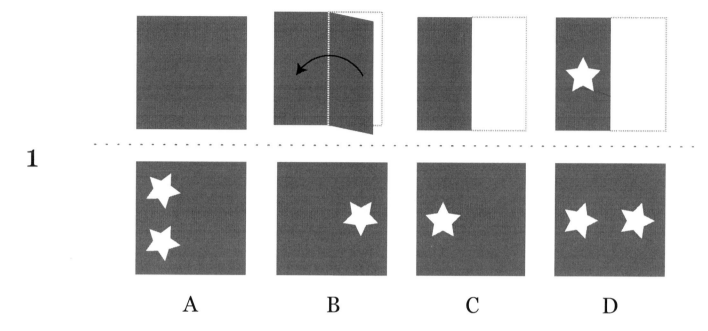

1

A   B   C   D

The paper in the top row is folded and cut as shown. Which paper in the bottom row is the result when the paper is unfolded?

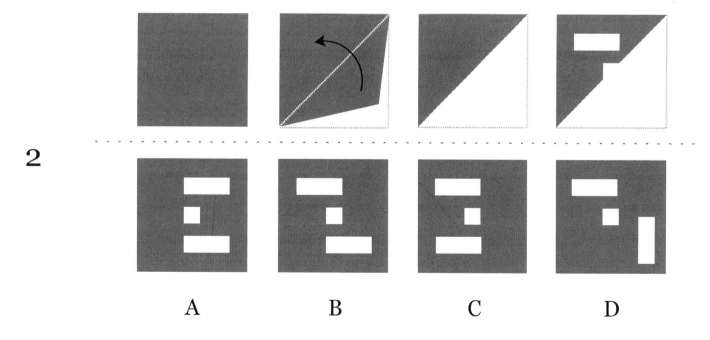

2

A   B   C   D

The paper in the top row is folded and cut as shown. Which paper in the bottom row is the result when the paper is unfolded?

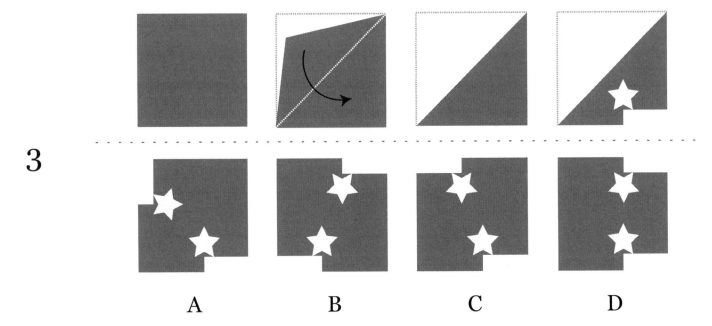

3

A   B   C   D

The paper in the top row is folded and cut as shown. Which paper in the bottom row is the result when the paper is unfolded?

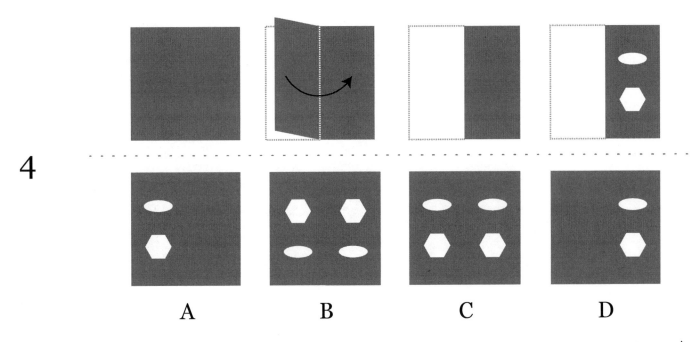

4

A   B   C   D

Paper Folding

The paper in the top row is folded and cut as shown. Which paper in the bottom row is the result when the paper is unfolded?

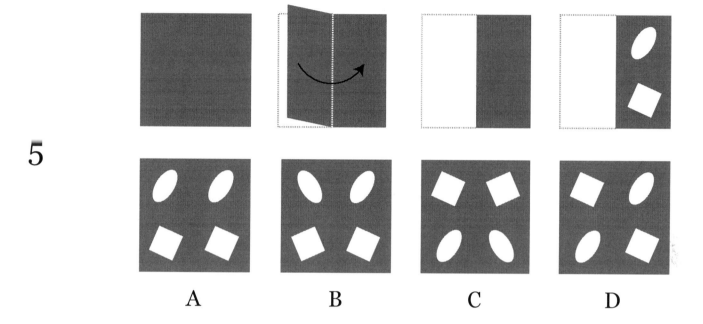

5

A   B   C   D

The paper in the top row is folded and cut as shown. Which paper in the bottom row is the result when the paper is unfolded?

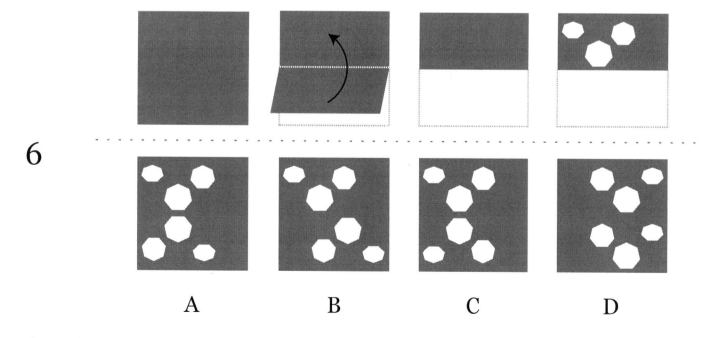

6

A   B   C   D

Paper Folding

The paper in the top row is folded and cut as shown. Which paper in the bottom row is the result when the paper is unfolded?

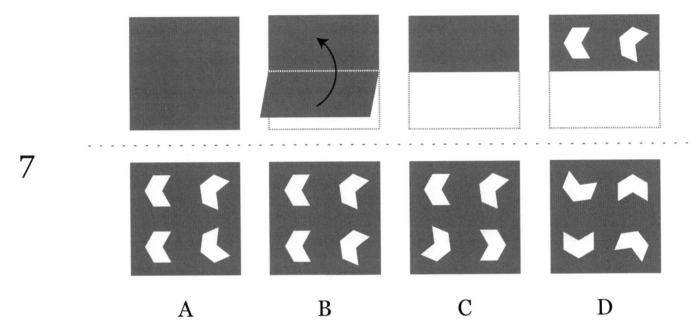

7

A   B   C   D

The paper in the top row is folded and cut as shown. Which paper in the bottom row is the result when the paper is unfolded?

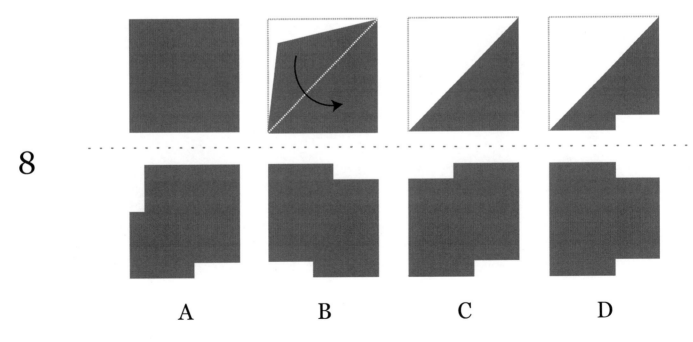

8

A   B   C   D

Paper Folding

The paper in the top row is folded and cut as shown. Which paper in the bottom row is the result when the paper is unfolded?

9

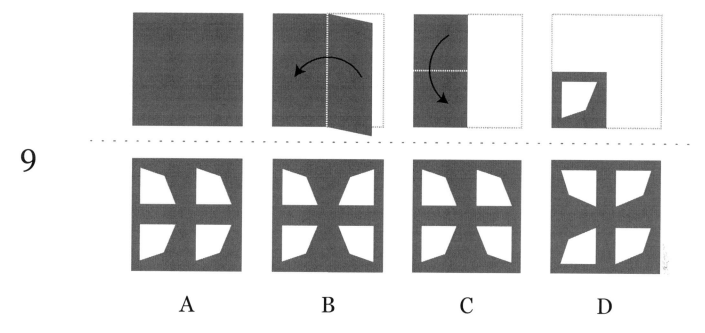

A   B   C   D

The paper in the top row is folded and cut as shown. Which paper in the bottom row is the result when the paper is unfolded?

10

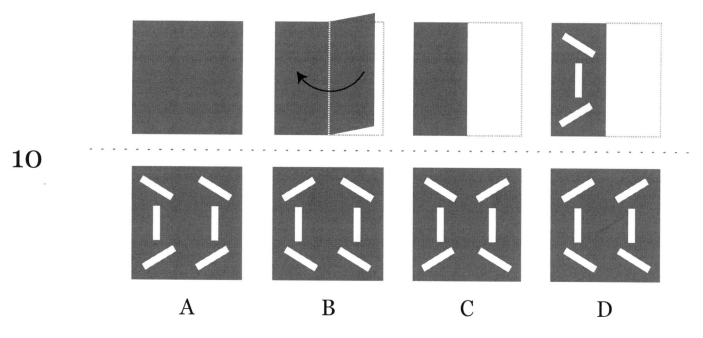

A   B   C   D

The paper in the top row is folded and cut as shown. Which paper in the bottom row is the result when the paper is unfolded?

11

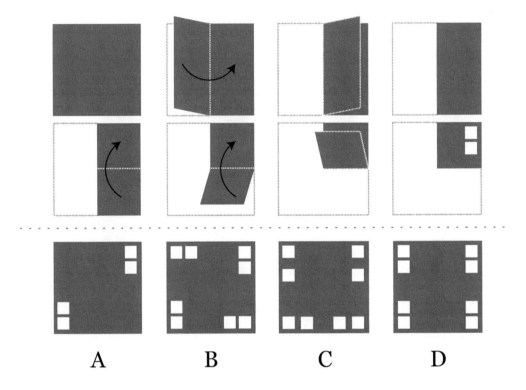

A   B   C   D

The paper in the top row is folded and cut as shown. Which paper in the bottom row is the result when the paper is unfolded?

12

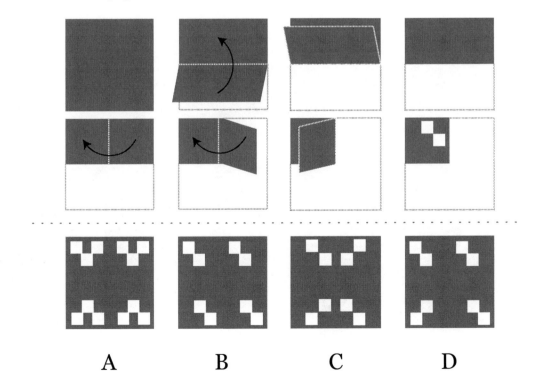

A   B   C   D

Paper Folding

The paper in the top row is folded and cut as shown. Which paper in the bottom row is the result when the paper is unfolded?

13

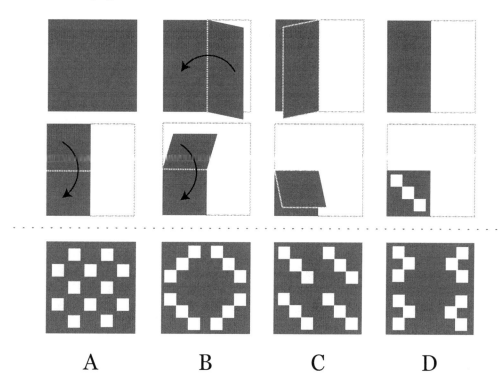

A   B   C   D

The paper in the top row is folded and cut as shown. Which paper in the bottom row is the result when the paper is unfolded?

14

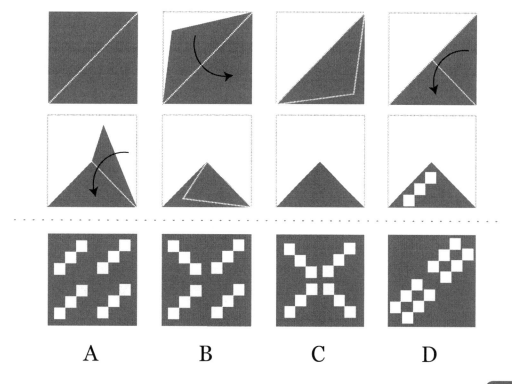

A   B   C   D

CogAT® Quantitative Battery

Number Analogies

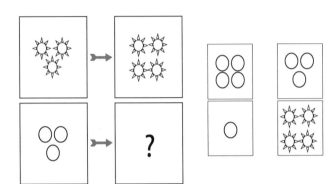

Number Series

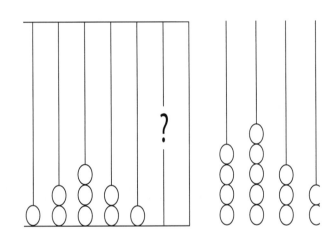

Number Puzzles

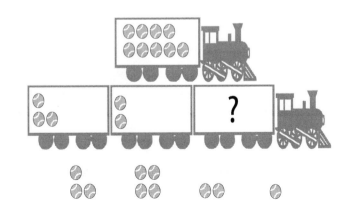

Number Analogies
Practice Questions

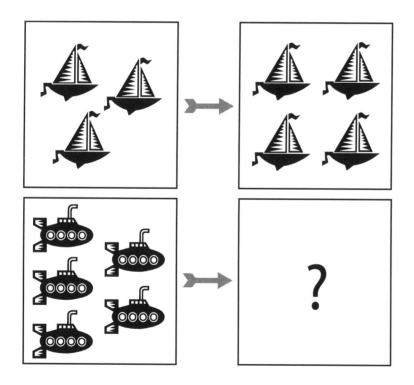

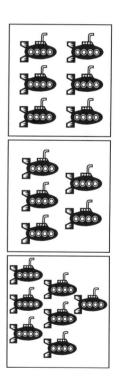

Number Analogies

Which image best fits in the box with the question mark?

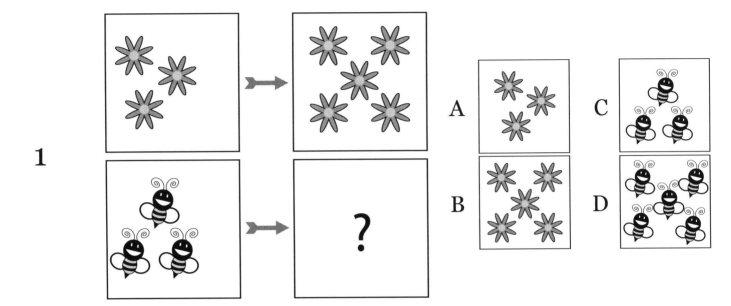

Which image best fits in the box with the question mark?

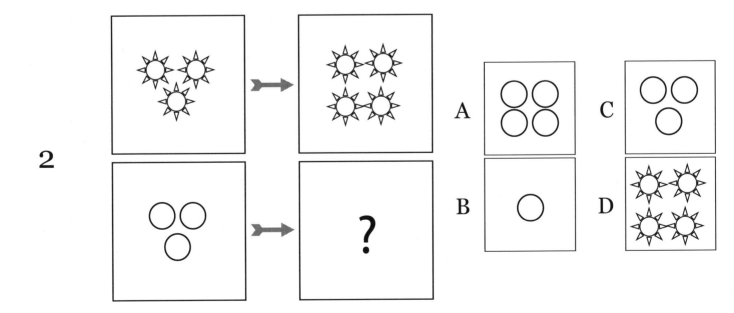

Gifted & Talented Test Prep Team

Number Analogies

Which image best fits in the box with the question mark?

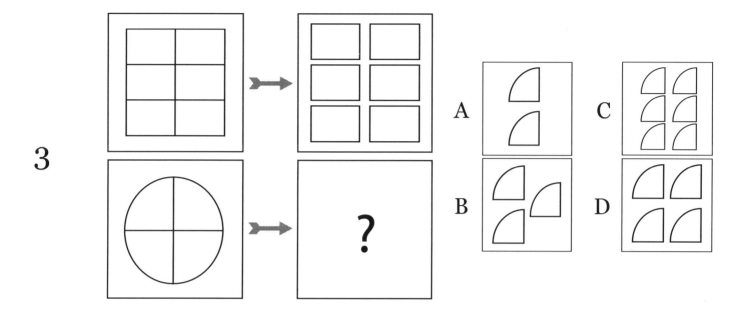

Which image best fits in the box with the question mark?

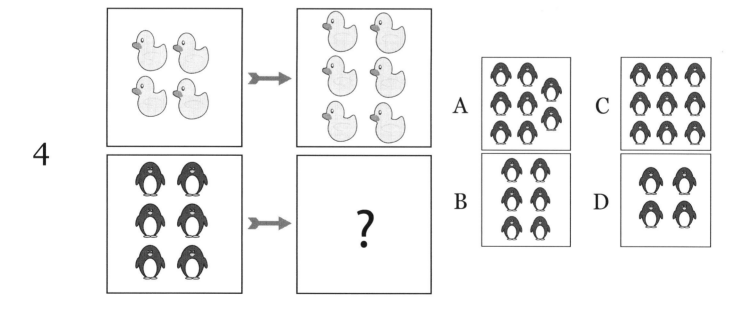

Number Analogies

Which image best fits in the box with the question mark?

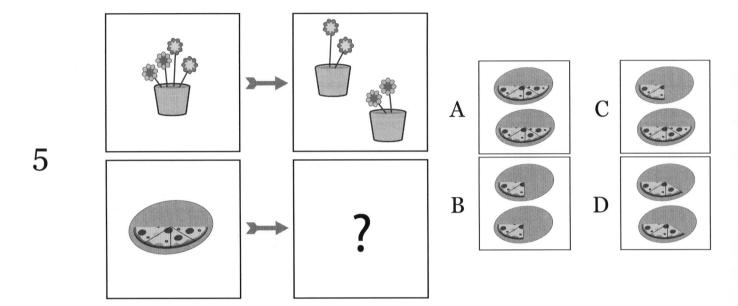

Which image best fits in the box with the question mark?

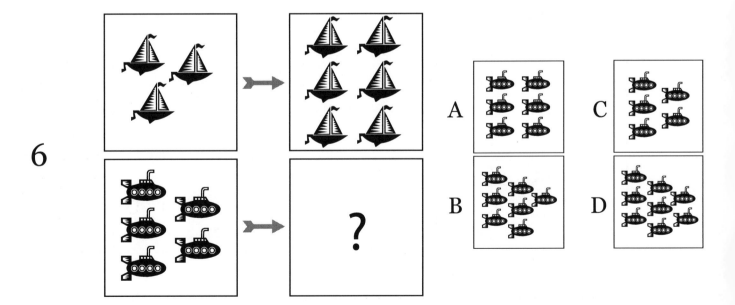

Number Analogies

Which image best fits in the box with the question mark?

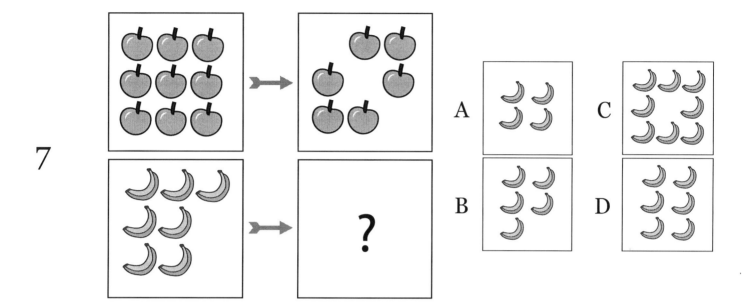

Which image best fits in the box with the question mark?

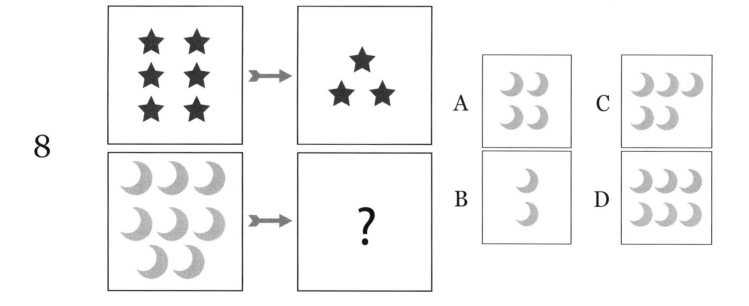

Number Analogies

Which image best fits in the box with the question mark?

9

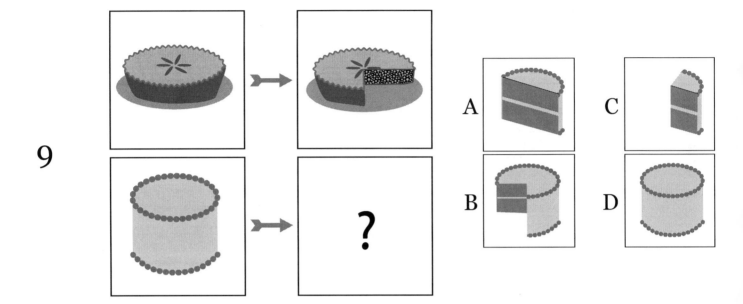

Which image best fits in the box with the question mark?

10

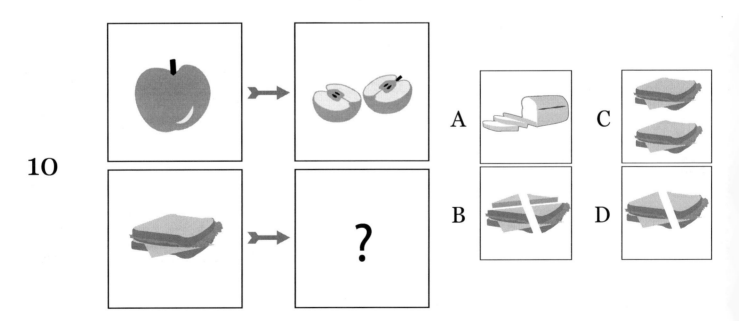

CogAT® Level 8 Test Prep Book   Gifted & Talented Test Prep Team

Number Analogies

Which image best fits in the box with the question mark?

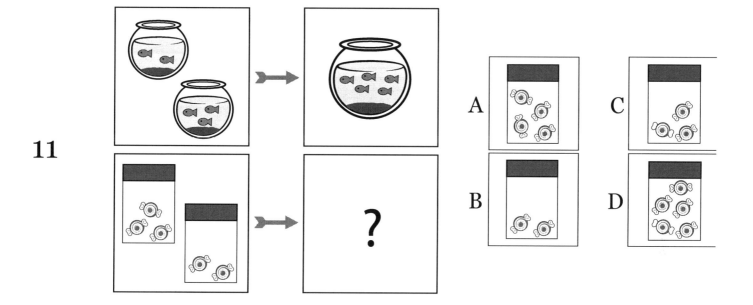

11

Which image best fits in the box with the question mark?

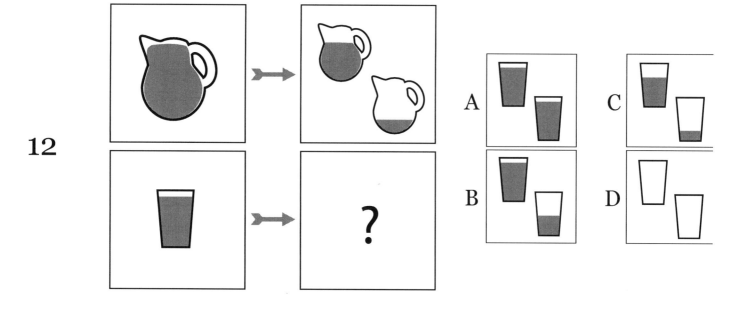

12

Number Analogies

Which image best fits in the box with the question mark?

13

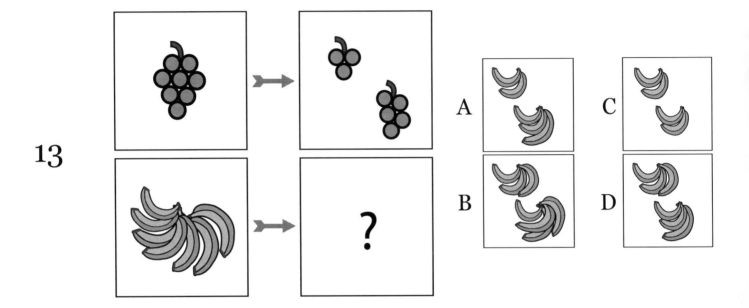

Which image best fits in the box with the question mark?

14

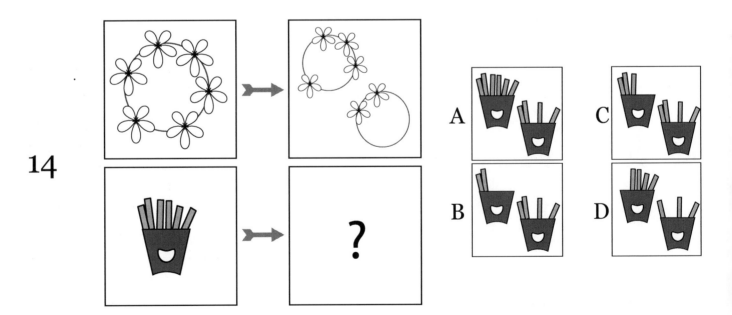

Which image best fits in the box with the question mark?

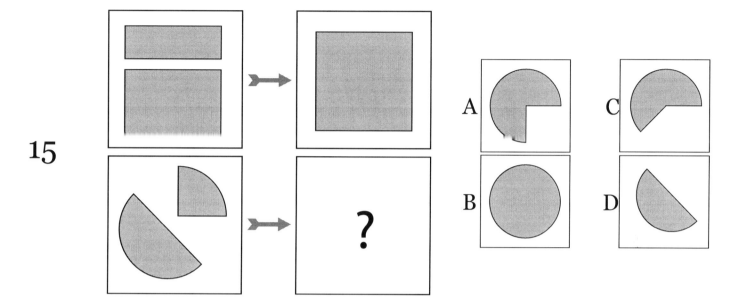

15

Which image best fits in the box with the question mark?

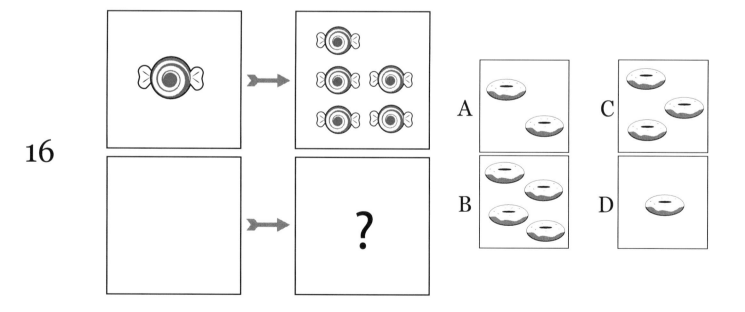

16

Which image best fits in the box with the question mark?

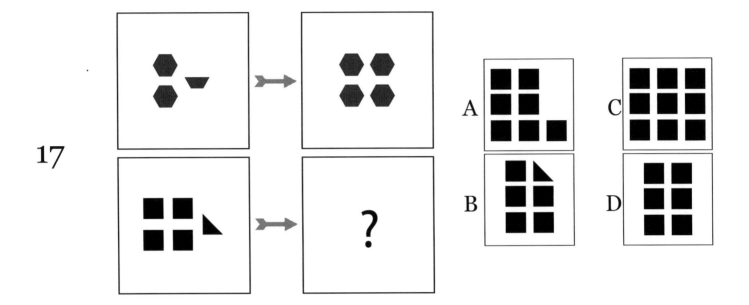

17

Which image best fits in the box with the question mark?

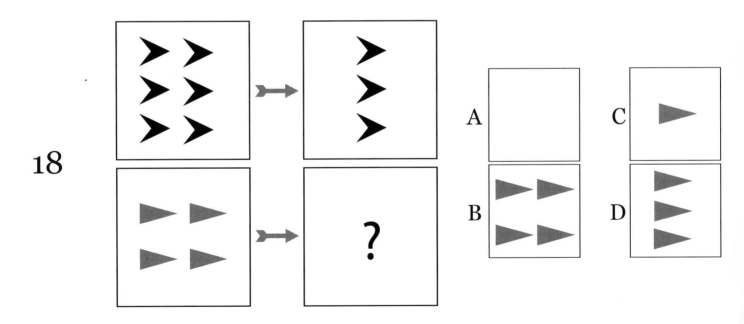

18

Number Series
Practice Questions

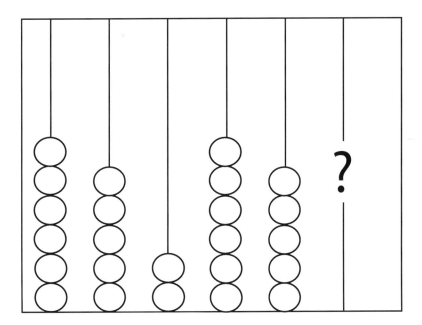

Number Series

Which picture goes in the box with the question mark?

1

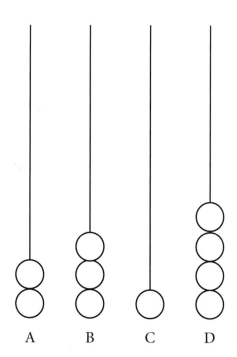

A   B   C   D

Which picture goes in the box with the question mark?

2

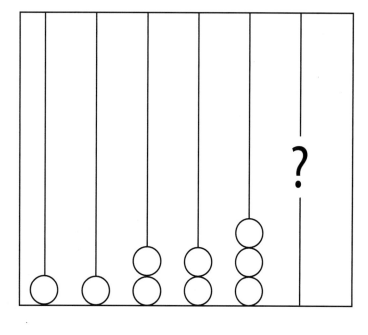

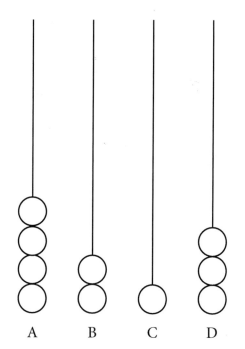

A   B   C   D

CogAT® Level 8 Test Prep Book   Gifted & Talented Test Prep Team

Which picture goes in the box with the question mark?

3

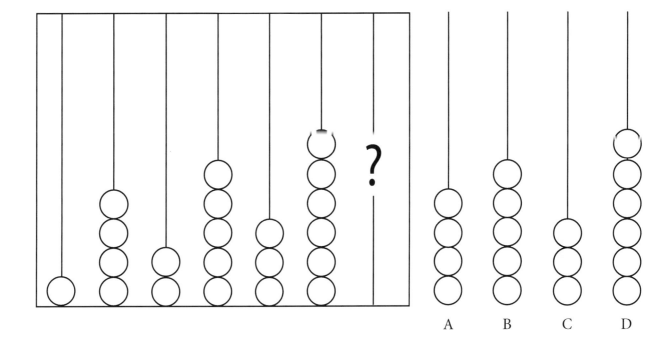

Which picture goes in the box with the question mark?

4

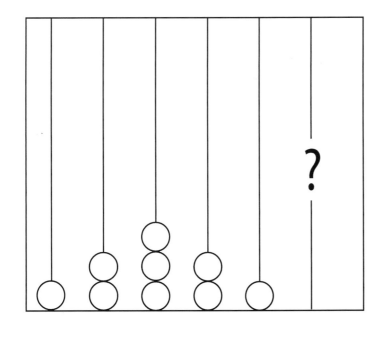 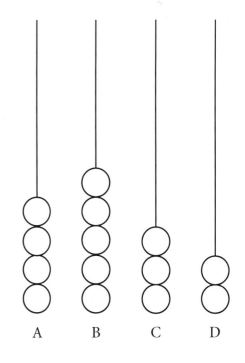

Which picture goes in the box with the question mark?

5

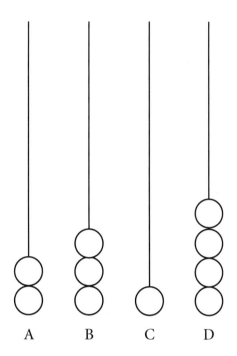

Which picture goes in the box with the question mark?

6

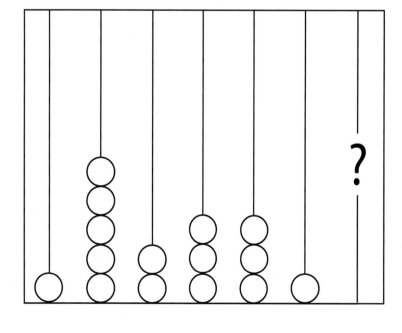
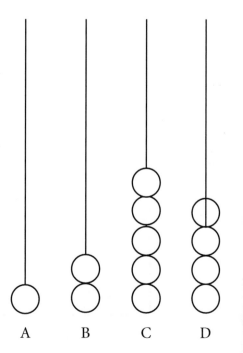

Which picture goes in the box with the question mark?

7

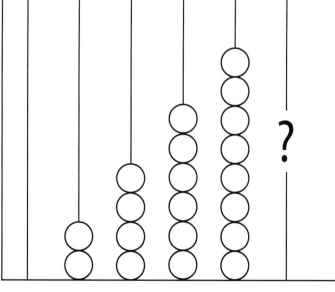
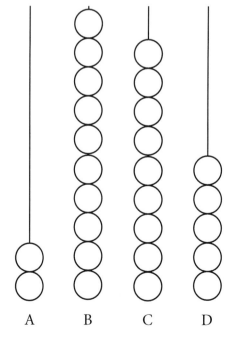

A   B   C   D

Which picture goes in the box with the question mark?

8

A   B   C   D

Number Series

Which picture goes in the box with the question mark?

9

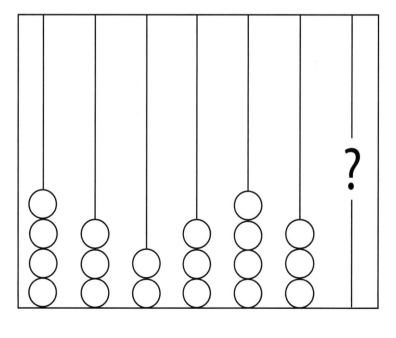

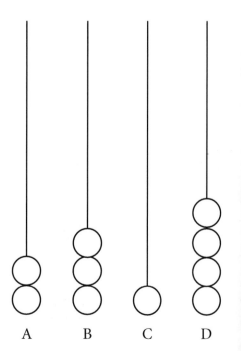

A   B   C   D

Which picture goes in the box with the question mark?

10

A   B   C   D

CogAT® Level 8 Test Prep Book   Gifted & Talented Test Prep Team

Which picture goes in the box with the question mark?

11

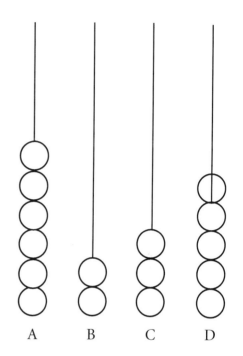

A   B   C   D

Which picture goes in the box with the question mark?

12

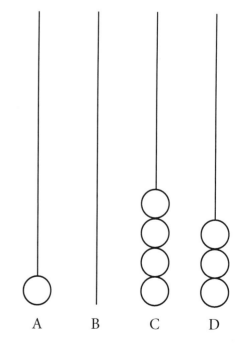

A   B   C   D

Which picture goes in the box with the question mark?

13

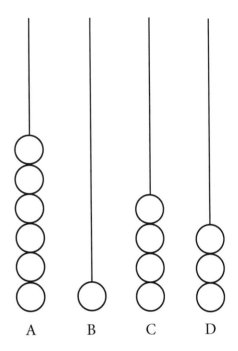

Which picture goes in the box with the question mark?

14

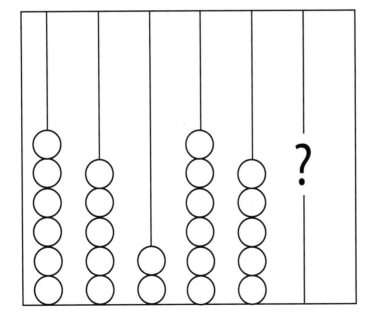
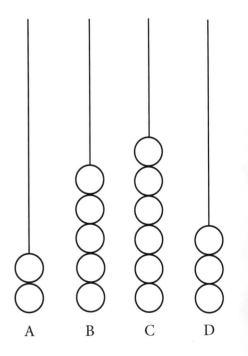

Which picture goes in the box with the question mark?

15

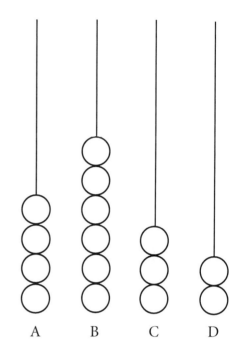

Which picture goes in the box with the question mark?

16

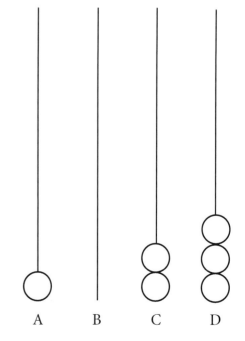

Which picture goes in the box with the question mark?

17

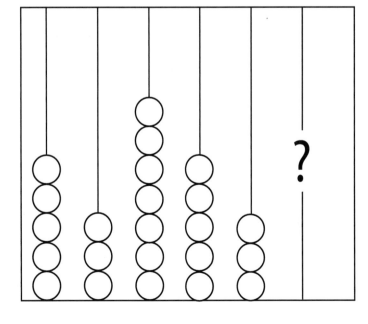

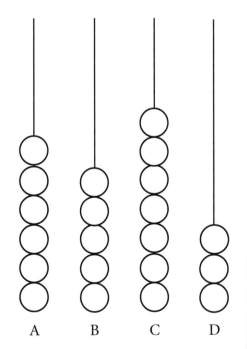

Which picture goes in the box with the question mark?

18

Number Puzzles
Practice Questions

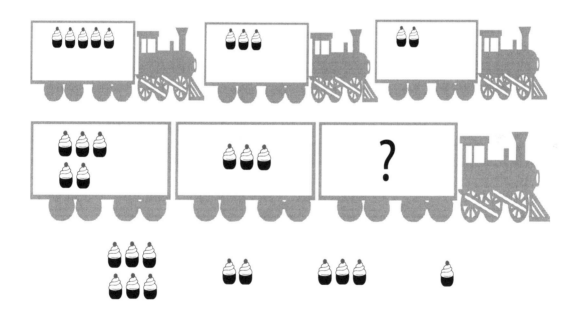

Number Puzzles

Which picture goes in the box with the question mark?

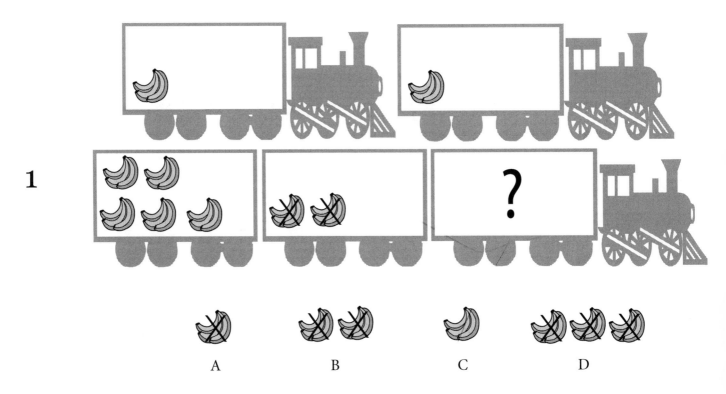

Which picture goes in the box with the question mark?

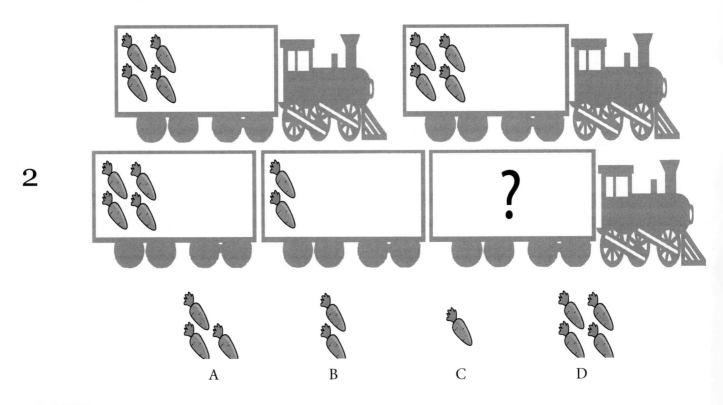

Number Puzzles

Which picture goes in the box with the question mark?

3

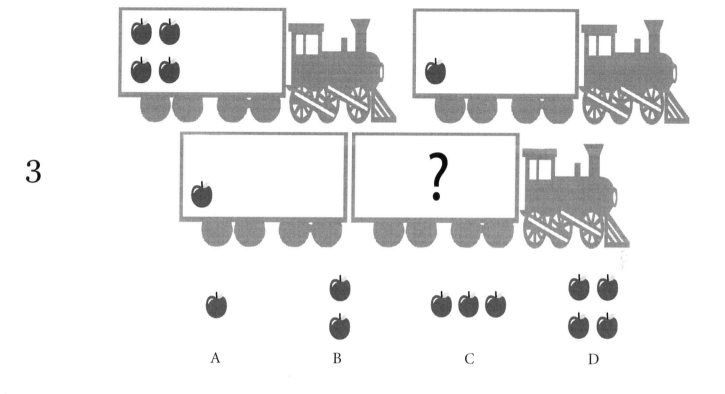

A　　　　B　　　　C　　　　D

Which picture goes in the box with the question mark?

4

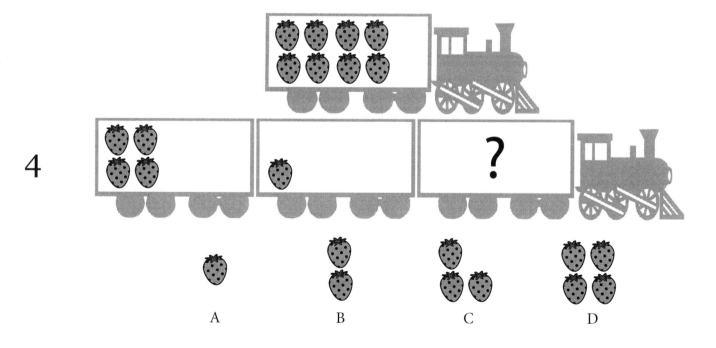

A　　　　B　　　　C　　　　D

Number Puzzles

Which picture goes in the box with the question mark?

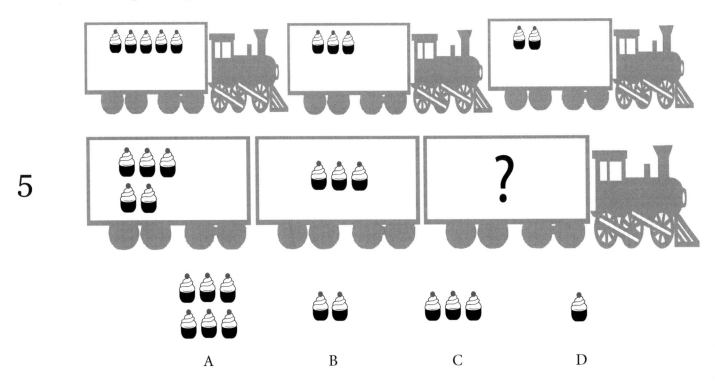

A   B   C   D

Which picture goes in the box with the question mark?

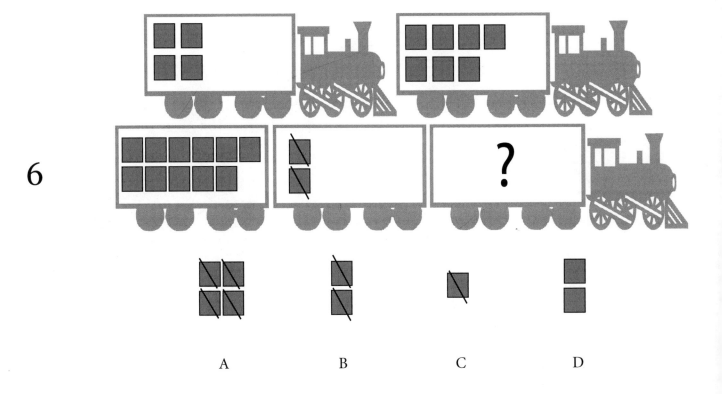

A   B   C   D

Number Puzzles

Which picture goes in the box with the question mark?

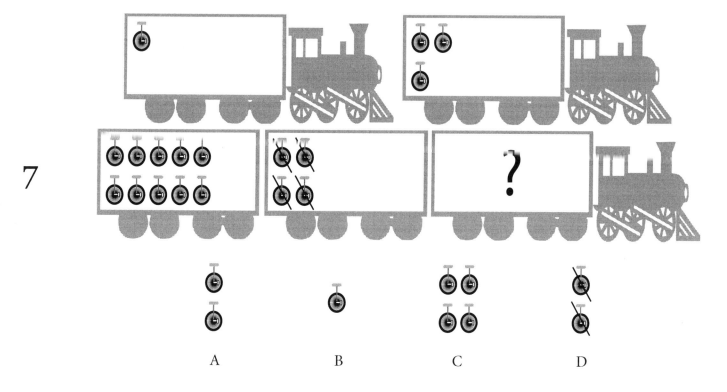

7

A   B   C   D

Which picture goes in the box with the question mark?

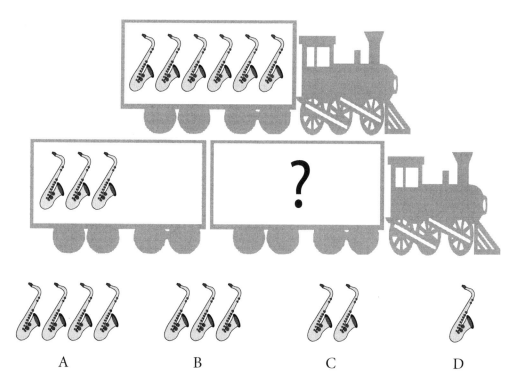

8

A   B   C   D

Number Puzzles

Which picture goes in the box with the question mark?

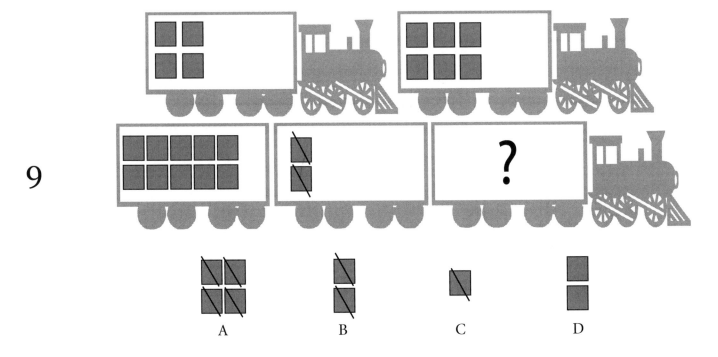

9

Which picture goes in the box with the question mark?

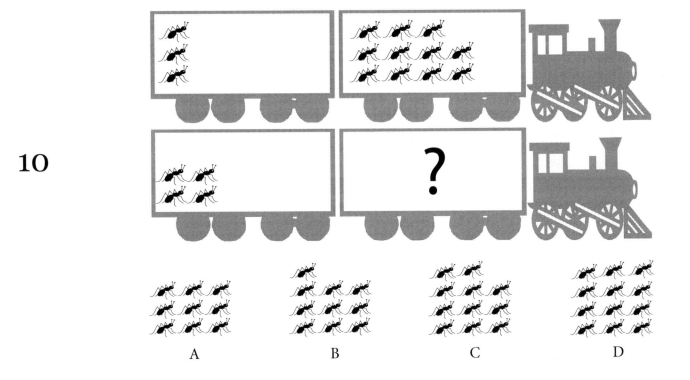

10

CogAT® Level 8 Test Prep Book   Gifted & Talented Test Prep Team

Number Puzzles

Which picture goes in the box with the question mark?

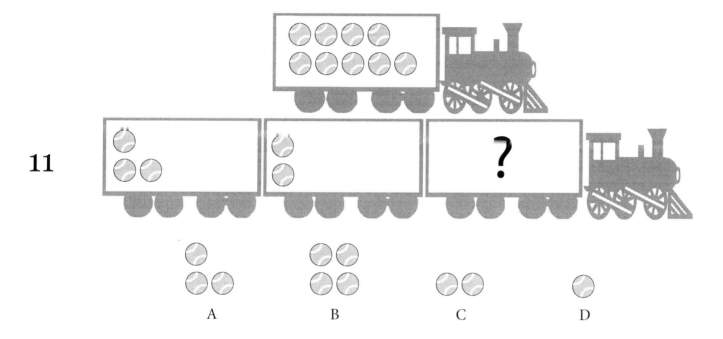

11

A   B   C   D

Which picture goes in the box with the question mark?

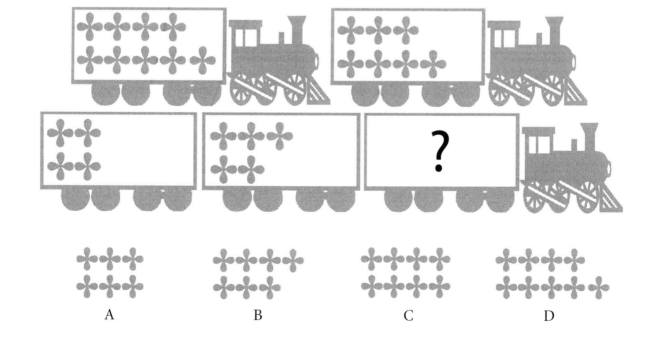

12

A   B   C   D

Number Puzzles

Which picture goes in the box with the question mark?

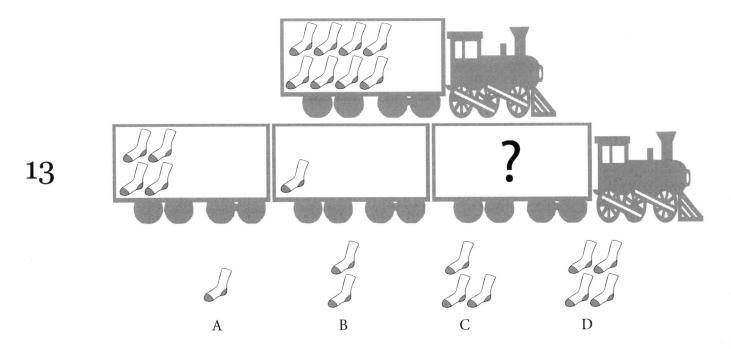

13

A   B   C   D

Which picture goes in the box with the question mark?

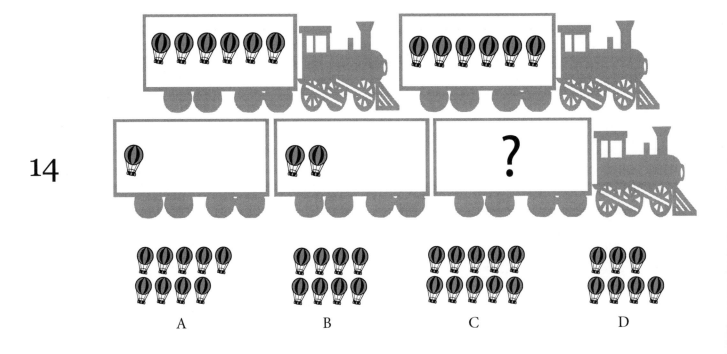

14

A   B   C   D

Test Answers
& Bubble Sheets

CogAT® Verbal Battery Answers

Number	Answer	Explanation
		**Sentence Completion**
1	C	
2	D	
3	C	
4	A	
5	D	
6	B	
7	B	
8	C	
9	C	
10	C	
11	D	
12	A	
13	A	
14	C	
15	A	
16	C	
17	D	
18	B	

Number	Answer	Explanation
		Picture Classification
1	B	
2	B	
3	A	
4	C	
5	B	
6	A	Sets of 2 items.
7	B	
8	D	
9	B	
10	B	
11	A	Camping gear/items needed to camp outside.
12	A	
13	A	
14	C	Items/animals/insects that can fly in sky.
15	B	Items to help people (who cannot walk) get around/ travel.
16	B	All electrical items. Items need to be plugged into electrical socket to work.
17	A	All items worn on bottom half of body.
18	C	All items made of metal.

CogAT® Verbal Battery Answers

Number	Answer	Explanation
		Picture Analogies
1	B	
2	B	
3	B	
4	A	
5	B	
6	A	
7	D	
8	A	
9	C	
10	C	
11	A	
12	D	
13	B	
14	A	
15	D	
16	B	
17	B	
18	B	

CogAT® Nonverbal Battery Answers

Number	Answer	Explanation
		Figure Matrices
1	B	
2	D	
3	A	Figure moves quarter turn to left.
4	B	
5	D	
6	D	
7	A	
8	A	
9	D	
10	C	
11	D	Outside shape moves quarter turn to left. Inside shape changes.
12	D	Square turns 1/4 turn to left. Colors are flipped.
13	B	
14	C	In top row, the shape's sides increase by 1. In bottom row, the points of the star increase by 1.
15	A	
16	B	
17	C	
18	D	In top row, 3 small black triangles become 2 triangles (1 large black triangle & 1 medium white inner triangle). Large white squares get smaller (but stay same amount & same color). In bottom row, 3 small white squares become large white outer square & medium black inner square. Larger black circles get smaller but stay the same amount (3 circles) & same color (black).

Number	Answer	Explanation
		Figure Classification
1	B	
2	B	
3	B	
4	C	
5	D	
6	B	
7	D	
8	A	
9	A	
10	C	Each of the shapes has 8 sides.
11	C	
12	C	Each of the shapes has 4 sides.
13	B	
14	D	
15	C	Each of the shapes has 6 sides.
16	A	Triangle points to cut-out corner, or the L-shape rotates with triangle in same place.
17	A	Star faces a flat edge, not a point.
18	D	

CogAT® Nonverbal Battery Answers

Number	Answer	Explanation
		Paper Folding
1	D	
2	D	
3	A	
4	C	
5	B	
6	C	
7	A	
8	A	
9	B	
10	C	
11	D	
12	C	
13	B	
14	D	

CogAT® Quantitative Battery Answers

Number	Answer	Explanation
		Number Analogies
1	D	2 items (flowers) were added to top row. 2 items (bees) must be added to bottom row, which adds up to 5 bees.
2	A	One item was added to top row. One item (circle) must be added to bottom row, which adds up to 4 circles.
3	D	
4	A	2 items were added to top row. 2 items (penguins) must be added to bottom row, which adds up to 8 penguins.
5	B	
6	D	3 items were added to top row. 3 items (submarines) must be added to bottom row, which adds up to 8 submarines.
7	A	3 items were subtracted from top row. 3 items (bananas) must be subtracted from bottom row, leaving 4 bananas.
8	C	3 items were subtracted from top row. 3 items (moons) must be subtracted from bottom row, leaving 5 moons.
9	B	
10	D	
11	D	
12	C	
13	B	
14	B	
15	A	
16	B	4 items were added to top row. 4 items (donuts) must be added to bottom row, which adds up to 4 donuts.
17	D	1.5 items were added to top row. 1.5 items (squares) must be added to bottom row, which adds up to 6 squares.
18	C	3 items were subtracted from top row. 3 items (arrows) must be subtracted from bottom row, leaving 1 arrow.

Number	Answer	Explanation
		Number Series
1	A	This is a pattern of four. The pattern is 4,3,2,3. It would then begin again.
2	D	The pattern is to repeat the number, then add one and then repeat the number: 1,1,2,2,3,3, and so on.
3	A	The 1st, 3rd & 5th rods (and thus 7th rod) increase by 1 bead. The 2nd, 4th & 6th rods also increase by 1 bead.
4	D	This is a pattern of four. The pattern is 1,2,3,2. It would then begin again.
5	A	This is a pattern of four. The pattern is 5,4,2,3. It would then begin again.
6	D	The 1st, 3rd & 5th (and thus 7th) rods add 1 bead. The 2nd, 4th & 6th rods subtract two beads.
7	B	This is a pattern of three. The pattern is 0,0,4. It would then begin again.
8	B	The pattern is to add 2 to each rod: 0,2,4,6,8, and so on....
9	B	The 1st, 3rd & 5th (and thus 7th) rods subtract 3 beads. The 2nd, 4th & 6th rods add one bead.
10	A	This is a pattern of four. The pattern is 4,3,2,3. It would then begin again.
11	D	This is a pattern of four. The pattern is 4,5,3,2. It would then begin again.
12	C	This is a pattern of four. The pattern is 2,4,0,1. It would then begin again.
13	D	The 1st, 3rd & 5th rods subtract 1 bead. The 2nd, 4th (and thus 6th rod) rods also add 1 bead.
14	A	This is a pattern of three. The pattern is 6,5,2. It would then begin again.
15	B	This is a pattern of three. The pattern is 4,3,6. It would then begin again.
16	A	The 1st, 3rd & 5th rods subtract one bead. The 2nd, 4th (& thus 6th) rods stay the same.
17	C	The 1st, 3rd & 5th rods subtract one bead. The 2nd, 4th (& thus 6th) rods add one bead.
18	C	This is a pattern of three. The pattern is 5,3,7. It would then begin again.

CogAT® Quantitative Battery Answers

Number	Answer	Explanation
		Number Puzzles
1	A	# of items in train carriage/s in top row must equal # of items in bottom row. "X'd out" item/s indicates "subtract item/s"
2	B	# of items in train carriage/s in top row must equal # of items in bottom row.
3	D	# of items in train carriage/s in top row must equal # of items in bottom row.
4	C	# of items in train carriage/s in top row must equal # of items in bottom row.
5	B	# of items in train carriage/s in top row must equal # of items in bottom row.
6	D	# of items in train carriage/s in top row must equal # of items in bottom row. "X'd out" item/s indicates "subtract item/s"
7	D	# of items in train carriage/s in top row must equal # of items in bottom row. "X'd out" item/s indicates "subtract item/s"
8	B	# of items in train carriage/s in top row must equal # of items in bottom row.
9	D	# of items in train carriage/s in top row must equal # of items in bottom row. "X'd out" item/s indicates "subtract item/s"
10	B	# of items in train carriage/s in top row must equal # of items in bottom row.
11	B	# of items in train carriage/s in top row must equal # of items in bottom row.
12	B	# of items in train carriage/s in top row must equal # of items in bottom row.
13	C	# of items in train carriage/s in top row must equal # of items in bottom row.
14	A	# of items in train carriage/s in top row must equal # of items in bottom row.

CogAT® Verbal Battery

Use a No. 2 Pencil
Fill in bubble completely.

Ⓐ ● Ⓒ Ⓓ

Name:_____   Date:_____

1. Ⓐ Ⓑ Ⓒ Ⓓ	1. Ⓐ Ⓑ Ⓒ Ⓓ	1. Ⓐ Ⓑ Ⓒ Ⓓ
2. Ⓐ Ⓑ Ⓒ Ⓓ	2. Ⓐ Ⓑ Ⓒ Ⓓ	2. Ⓐ Ⓑ Ⓒ Ⓓ
3. Ⓐ Ⓑ Ⓒ Ⓓ	3. Ⓐ Ⓑ Ⓒ Ⓓ	3. Ⓐ Ⓑ Ⓒ Ⓓ
4. Ⓐ Ⓑ Ⓒ Ⓓ	4. Ⓐ Ⓑ Ⓒ Ⓓ	4. Ⓐ Ⓑ Ⓒ Ⓓ
5. Ⓐ Ⓑ Ⓒ Ⓓ	5. Ⓐ Ⓑ Ⓒ Ⓓ	5. Ⓐ Ⓑ Ⓒ Ⓓ
6. Ⓐ Ⓑ Ⓒ Ⓓ	6. Ⓐ Ⓑ Ⓒ Ⓓ	6. Ⓐ Ⓑ Ⓒ Ⓓ
7. Ⓐ Ⓑ Ⓒ Ⓓ	7. Ⓐ Ⓑ Ⓒ Ⓓ	7. Ⓐ Ⓑ Ⓒ Ⓓ
8. Ⓐ Ⓑ Ⓒ Ⓓ	8. Ⓐ Ⓑ Ⓒ Ⓓ	8. Ⓐ Ⓑ Ⓒ Ⓓ
9. Ⓐ Ⓑ Ⓒ Ⓓ	9. Ⓐ Ⓑ Ⓒ Ⓓ	9. Ⓐ Ⓑ Ⓒ Ⓓ
10. Ⓐ Ⓑ Ⓒ Ⓓ	10. Ⓐ Ⓑ Ⓒ Ⓓ	10. Ⓐ Ⓑ Ⓒ Ⓓ
11. Ⓐ Ⓑ Ⓒ Ⓓ	11. Ⓐ Ⓑ Ⓒ Ⓓ	11. Ⓐ Ⓑ Ⓒ Ⓓ
12. Ⓐ Ⓑ Ⓒ Ⓓ	12. Ⓐ Ⓑ Ⓒ Ⓓ	12. Ⓐ Ⓑ Ⓒ Ⓓ
13. Ⓐ Ⓑ Ⓒ Ⓓ	13. Ⓐ Ⓑ Ⓒ Ⓓ	13. Ⓐ Ⓑ Ⓒ Ⓓ
14. Ⓐ Ⓑ Ⓒ Ⓓ	14. Ⓐ Ⓑ Ⓒ Ⓓ	14. Ⓐ Ⓑ Ⓒ Ⓓ
15. Ⓐ Ⓑ Ⓒ Ⓓ	15. Ⓐ Ⓑ Ⓒ Ⓓ	15. Ⓐ Ⓑ Ⓒ Ⓓ
16. Ⓐ Ⓑ Ⓒ Ⓓ	16. Ⓐ Ⓑ Ⓒ Ⓓ	16. Ⓐ Ⓑ Ⓒ Ⓓ
17. Ⓐ Ⓑ Ⓒ Ⓓ	17. Ⓐ Ⓑ Ⓒ Ⓓ	17. Ⓐ Ⓑ Ⓒ Ⓓ
18. Ⓐ Ⓑ Ⓒ Ⓓ	18. Ⓐ Ⓑ Ⓒ Ⓓ	18. Ⓐ Ⓑ Ⓒ Ⓓ

CogAT® Nonverbal Battery

Use a No. 2 Pencil
Fill in bubble completely.
Ⓐ ● Ⓒ Ⓓ

Name:_____ Date:_____

1. Ⓐ Ⓑ Ⓒ Ⓓ	1. Ⓐ Ⓑ Ⓒ Ⓓ	1. Ⓐ Ⓑ Ⓒ Ⓓ
2. Ⓐ Ⓑ Ⓒ Ⓓ	2. Ⓐ Ⓑ Ⓒ Ⓓ	2. Ⓐ Ⓑ Ⓒ Ⓓ
3. Ⓐ Ⓑ Ⓒ Ⓓ	3. Ⓐ Ⓑ Ⓒ Ⓓ	3. Ⓐ Ⓑ Ⓒ Ⓓ
4. Ⓐ Ⓑ Ⓒ Ⓓ	4. Ⓐ Ⓑ Ⓒ Ⓓ	4. Ⓐ Ⓑ Ⓒ Ⓓ
5. Ⓐ Ⓑ Ⓒ Ⓓ	5. Ⓐ Ⓑ Ⓒ Ⓓ	5. Ⓐ Ⓑ Ⓒ Ⓓ
6. Ⓐ Ⓑ Ⓒ Ⓓ	6. Ⓐ Ⓑ Ⓒ Ⓓ	6. Ⓐ Ⓑ Ⓒ Ⓓ
7. Ⓐ Ⓑ Ⓒ Ⓓ	7. Ⓐ Ⓑ Ⓒ Ⓓ	7. Ⓐ Ⓑ Ⓒ Ⓓ
8. Ⓐ Ⓑ Ⓒ Ⓓ	8. Ⓐ Ⓑ Ⓒ Ⓓ	8. Ⓐ Ⓑ Ⓒ Ⓓ
9. Ⓐ Ⓑ Ⓒ Ⓓ	9. Ⓐ Ⓑ Ⓒ Ⓓ	9. Ⓐ Ⓑ Ⓒ Ⓓ
10. Ⓐ Ⓑ Ⓒ Ⓓ	10. Ⓐ Ⓑ Ⓒ Ⓓ	10. Ⓐ Ⓑ Ⓒ Ⓓ
11. Ⓐ Ⓑ Ⓒ Ⓓ	11. Ⓐ Ⓑ Ⓒ Ⓓ	11. Ⓐ Ⓑ Ⓒ Ⓓ
12. Ⓐ Ⓑ Ⓒ Ⓓ	12. Ⓐ Ⓑ Ⓒ Ⓓ	12. Ⓐ Ⓑ Ⓒ Ⓓ
13. Ⓐ Ⓑ Ⓒ Ⓓ	13. Ⓐ Ⓑ Ⓒ Ⓓ	13. Ⓐ Ⓑ Ⓒ Ⓓ
14. Ⓐ Ⓑ Ⓒ Ⓓ	14. Ⓐ Ⓑ Ⓒ Ⓓ	14. Ⓐ Ⓑ Ⓒ Ⓓ
15. Ⓐ Ⓑ Ⓒ Ⓓ	15. Ⓐ Ⓑ Ⓒ Ⓓ	
16. Ⓐ Ⓑ Ⓒ Ⓓ	16. Ⓐ Ⓑ Ⓒ Ⓓ	
17. Ⓐ Ⓑ Ⓒ Ⓓ	17. Ⓐ Ⓑ Ⓒ Ⓓ	
18. Ⓐ Ⓑ Ⓒ Ⓓ	18. Ⓐ Ⓑ Ⓒ Ⓓ	

CogAT® Quantitative Battery

Use a No. 2 Pencil
Fill in bubble completely.

Ⓐ ● Ⓒ Ⓓ

Name:_____   Date:_____

1. Ⓐ Ⓑ Ⓒ Ⓓ	1. Ⓐ Ⓑ Ⓒ Ⓓ	1. Ⓐ Ⓑ Ⓒ Ⓓ
2. Ⓐ Ⓑ Ⓒ Ⓓ	2. Ⓐ Ⓑ Ⓒ Ⓓ	2. Ⓐ Ⓑ Ⓒ Ⓓ
3. Ⓐ Ⓑ Ⓒ Ⓓ	3. Ⓐ Ⓑ Ⓒ Ⓓ	3. Ⓐ Ⓑ Ⓒ Ⓓ
4. Ⓐ Ⓑ Ⓒ Ⓓ	4. Ⓐ Ⓑ Ⓒ Ⓓ	4. Ⓐ Ⓑ Ⓒ Ⓓ
5. Ⓐ Ⓑ Ⓒ Ⓓ	5. Ⓐ Ⓑ Ⓒ Ⓓ	5. Ⓐ Ⓑ Ⓒ Ⓓ
6. Ⓐ Ⓑ Ⓒ Ⓓ	6. Ⓐ Ⓑ Ⓒ Ⓓ	6. Ⓐ Ⓑ Ⓒ Ⓓ
7. Ⓐ Ⓑ Ⓒ Ⓓ	7. Ⓐ Ⓑ Ⓒ Ⓓ	7. Ⓐ Ⓑ Ⓒ Ⓓ
8. Ⓐ Ⓑ Ⓒ Ⓓ	8. Ⓐ Ⓑ Ⓒ Ⓓ	8. Ⓐ Ⓑ Ⓒ Ⓓ
9. Ⓐ Ⓑ Ⓒ Ⓓ	9. Ⓐ Ⓑ Ⓒ Ⓓ	9. Ⓐ Ⓑ Ⓒ Ⓓ
10. Ⓐ Ⓑ Ⓒ Ⓓ	10. Ⓐ Ⓑ Ⓒ Ⓓ	10. Ⓐ Ⓑ Ⓒ Ⓓ
11. Ⓐ Ⓑ Ⓒ Ⓓ	11. Ⓐ Ⓑ Ⓒ Ⓓ	11. Ⓐ Ⓑ Ⓒ Ⓓ
12. Ⓐ Ⓑ Ⓒ Ⓓ	12. Ⓐ Ⓑ Ⓒ Ⓓ	12. Ⓐ Ⓑ Ⓒ Ⓓ
13. Ⓐ Ⓑ Ⓒ Ⓓ	13. Ⓐ Ⓑ Ⓒ Ⓓ	13. Ⓐ Ⓑ Ⓒ Ⓓ
14. Ⓐ Ⓑ Ⓒ Ⓓ	14. Ⓐ Ⓑ Ⓒ Ⓓ	14. Ⓐ Ⓑ Ⓒ Ⓓ
15. Ⓐ Ⓑ Ⓒ Ⓓ	15. Ⓐ Ⓑ Ⓒ Ⓓ	
16. Ⓐ Ⓑ Ⓒ Ⓓ	16. Ⓐ Ⓑ Ⓒ Ⓓ	
17. Ⓐ Ⓑ Ⓒ Ⓓ	17. Ⓐ Ⓑ Ⓒ Ⓓ	
18. Ⓐ Ⓑ Ⓒ Ⓓ	18. Ⓐ Ⓑ Ⓒ Ⓓ	

Made in the USA
Monee, IL
26 February 2023